HORSE RACING IN BEVERLEY AND YORKSHIRE

(Left to Right) Lord John Oaksey - John Sexton - John Francombe -
Author Ken Brooke - at a fundraising dinner for
the Injured Jockeys Fund

KEN BROOKE

First published in Great Britain in 2016 by Black Tree Publishing

ISBN: 978-0-9955081-0-1

Design and Production by Black Tree Publishing, Hull
Gemini House, Lee Smith Street Hull HU9 1SD
Telephone: 01482 328677

Printed by: Fisk Printers, Hull
Cover photographs courtesy of The Hull Daily Mail
Photographs taken: Front 1989, Reverse Top 1975,
Reverse Bottom 1968

INTRODUCTION

The Sport of Kings has always been in my blood, and nothing gives me greater pleasure than to read or discuss horse racing. And while the exploits of the likes of the unbeaten *Frankel* have left me and many enthusiasts around the world amazed with his performances, particular when he won the Juddmonte Stakes, at York right here in Yorkshire in such convincing style. However it is the stories of yesteryear that intrigue me the most, particularly in Yorkshire, when jockeys, trainers and horses moved about the Country without the aid of a modern vehicle or road transport system. Today it is not unusual to see jockeys riding at three meetings in one day, and those involved in the jockeys Championship are literally flying about from one course to another. In past days, when to be champion trainer or jockey, must have been a considerable achievement, just to get from one meeting to another would certainly have caused today's jockeys agent's a logistical nightmare. And whilst it is unwise to live in the past, it really is intriguing to learn how the horse racing world ever managed to cope with the monumental difficulties that presented themselves both on and off the racecourses. What is for certain, that just like any other sport or life in general, in by-gone days, more characters could be found, and many of them could be found in Yorkshire, possible because it is the largest County and the best in the United Kingdom.

BIBLIOGRAPHY AND THANKS

Grateful thanks go to the following:- Jill Banks, Joyce and Mark Birch, Ian Balding, Jack Berry M.B.E, Dale Gibson, Steve Lawes, John Chapleo, Hilary Jack, Paul Thorpe, Graham Orange, John Mooney, Pat & Mary Rohan, Paul Downey, Ron Grantham, Alan English, Judith Cutts, Christine and Robin Moverley, Mrs Anne Henson, Chris Walker, Malcolm Tomlinson, the staff at Beverley Treasure House and Library, Hull daily Mail, Beverley Guardian, Wikipedia, Queen's Jockey by W.H.Carr, Malton Memories and I'Anson Triumphs, Yorkshire East Riding by J.Fairfax Blakeborough, Andy at Fisk Printers plus many other friends, and fellow racing enthusiasts for all their help and contributions.

PHOTOGRAPHS

I am extremely grateful to the Hull Daily Mail, Beverley Guardian and Chris Walker for the use of all the photographs illustrated in this book.

ABOUT THE AUTHOR

Ken was born in Kingston-upon Hull during the worst of the blitz of World War 2. After the war his family, took a keen interest in horse racing and in particular the betting side, albeit only for small stakes. In those days it was not easy to place a bet and they were obliged to place their bets via a bookies runner, a person who collected bets for the bookmaker on a cash only basis. Each bet was written on a scrap of paper, and passed to a 'runner' who waited at a certain point each day. The betting in this way was illegal and the 'runner' and the bookmaker were frequently arrested by the police.

His first experience of 'live' racing came when the family took him to Beverley or York races. They always made for the free enclosure or the cheap ring, to bet and watch the days racing. It was here that Ken became enthralled with the events of the day; he was totally fascinated by the cheering crowds, jockey boards, the Tic-Tac men waving their arms furiously to their colleagues in other parts of the course. Ken, was also present at the Dinner in 1990 when Beverley racecourse celebrated it's 300 years of racing.

What also fascinated him were the racecourse tipsters like Ras Prince Monolulo, who often ventured to York for the 'big' meetings. Prince Monolulo came to this Country from his birth place of St Croix, Danish West Indies in 1902 he dressed very colourful with a plume of feathers adorning his head, his best used and well known of his phrases was the cry "I gotta a horse" and was the best known tipster on the racecourses. He died in the Middlesex hospital in 1965 at the age of 84.

Ironically Ken later joined the Constabulary, but still continued to be enthralled by the Sport of Kings and he was so pleased when his duties took him back to Beverley racecourse to man the Police Office situated under the best stand. In the 1990's he was particularly pleased to organise Dinners in aid of the Injured Jockeys Fund, when he invited the likes of Lord John Oaksey and John Francome to visit Beverley and they kindly gave the after dinner speeches. He even persuaded Lord Oaksey to be the President of the then Beverley Racing Club, who's members met each month to listen to the views of a racing personality. Ken continued these Fund raising efforts after his retirement from the Constabulary.

He has been involved in a number of Partnerships in racehorses, including those with Maurice Camacho, Maurice Avison, Neville Bycroft, Mary Reveley, and Brian Rothwell who trained at Musley Bank, Malton, North Yorkshire, the stable now occupied by Richard Fahey. Brian was responsible in providing the first ever winner for the Three County Partnership. Further success came latterly when David O'Meara trained *Elusive Bonus* for the Partnership to win a total of five races for them. The filly also provided a first ever win for David Bergin in England, for this likeable Irish born apprentice, when winning at Redcar on the 23rd June 2012 and the same partnership followed up with a further memorable victory at the author's local course of Beverley three days later. David is now back in Ireland and is employed by Aidan O'Brian.

In the new Years Honours List of 2015 Ken was delighted to hear that he had been honoured by the award of the British Empire Medal for his work in the village of Leconfield and for his fund raising efforts in the local community together with fund raising efforts for the Injured Jockey's Fund, particularly for the Jack Berry House, recently opened in Malton, North Yorkshire.

APOLOGIES

Whilst I have tried to include as much information as possible, it is inevitable that I have missed some incident, jockey, trainer or other items from my notes, I do hope you will forgive me if I have, but after almost four years of research it is time to print off these memories and stories. I do hope that you enjoy them.

RACING AT BEVERLEY AND IN YORKSHIRE

In Yorkshire, we have, over the years had some wonderful characters grace the turf, not surprising, when you realise, for example, that the first recorded race meeting held at Beverley was six years after the birth of one of England's, nay the worlds greatest seaman, explorer, and cartographer, Yorkshire born and bred Captain James Cook.

So before most of the modern world was even discovered, Beverley began racing in 1734 and continues today on Beverley's beloved Westwood.

And, who would believe that in 1834 just 100 years later a rule was introduced in Newmarket that the official birthday of all horses would be deemed to be the first of January regardless of when it was born. That means that a foal born in January would have a three month advantage of one born in March the same year. A rule, that of course, still exists today.

The magnificent Beverley Minster and the nearby Westwood are without doubt the jewels in the crown of this East Yorkshire town of Beverley. It is due largely thanks to two Archbishops, that the Westwood today, is not covered in housing estates, shops or schools. Some say it was Archbishop Wickwane who in 1280 granted the soil and rights of pasturage to the Burgesses of Beverley, or was it the Archbishop Neville who made the same grant a hundred years later in 1380. What is apparent, those living today are eternally grateful to these far sighted gentlemen as the area remains one of only a few parks of Beverley to remain virtually unchanged. The Westwood is an area of 1174 acres of common land and stands high above the ancient market town of Beverley with magnificent views over the Minster and St Mary's church.

The whole area is used, by so many for recreational activities, and one of them, horse racing, was probably held at the location long before any organised racing took place. It is believed that many impromptu horse racing matches were held on the Westwood. In 1712 horse racing was seen on the Hurn (part of the Westwood) on September 9th to the 11th. By the middle of the century these were moved to the Whitsun. The Racing Calendar recorded horse racing on the Westwood in June 1734, and in that year as for many years after, cock-fighting was part of the proceedings.

The first Clerk of the Course was a Robert Norton; he was also the landlord of the Rose and Crown Inn where the race committee held their initial meetings. Later the Race Executive moved their Headquarters to the Tiger Inn, which in those days was situated in North Bar Street, Beverley.

In 1767 a subscription list was opened for the building of a permanent grand stand on the Westwood, known locally as the Hurn. The cost of the building was in excess of £1000 and this was defrayed by the issue of 300 silver free admission badges. Recently two of these badges came up for auction at a Driffield sale-room.

Owners in those days appreciated winning trophy's particularly 'cups', so in 1770 the racing executive included a race for "The Gold Cup" and was soon known as the Yorkshire Classic race and this trophy became a much coveted prize.

The Holderness Hunt staged National Hunt racing at Beverley between 1828 and 1839. But it did not appear to have been popular with the paying public, and was soon dropped.

It is interesting to note that the Gold Cup in 1839 was won by the five year old *Melbourne*, ridden by the then famous East Yorkshire jockey Slim Templeman. *Melbourne* was bred locally at Carnaby by a Mr J Robinson who in those days was a tenant farmer. He was trained at Beverley so the locals were able to celebrate a truly memorable victory. At stud *Melbourne* proved very successful and twice headed the list as the leading sire in the Country. One of his offspring was *Blink Bonny* a filly, *Blink Bonny* was owned and trained by the Malton based trainer William I'Anson, which won the Bishop Burton Stakes at Beverley in 1856, and the following season won the Derby and the Oaks. She was the 5-4 favourite to win the St Leger, however she could only finish 4th behind the John Scott owned and trained *Imperieuse.* It was widely believed at the time that her jockey John 'Jack' Charlton had deliberately pulled her, particularly as the following day, she carried ten pounds more weight, and won the Park Hill Stakes by six lengths and in a faster time than *Imperieuse* had won the St Leger. This prompted a very large crowd to demonstrate their feelings towards the connections of the filly. The incident came to be known as the "Blink *Bonny* riot".

Blink Bonny died at eight years of age whilst giving birth to *Breadalbane,* strangely enough her jockey John Charlton died of consumption only a few months later.

At the race meeting of June 1904 a real tragedy occurred at the bend leading to the straight, known as Hudson's Corner. Police Constable Arthur Kirby who was on special duty near the bend, saw a young woman, later to be identified as a Miss Susan Michael. She was a spinster of 57 years of age and was housekeeper to Mr J. Willis Mills, the then town clerk of Beverley. She apparently often visited the area to watch the racing, as PC Kirby saw her she began to walk across the course, just as a field of about 13 or 14 runners were negotiating the bend. The officer called out a warning to the lady but she obviously didn't hear him. So he rushed over to her and caught hold of her arm to drag her away. However the runners were almost upon them and the officer was struck on his shoulder by one of the runners, which sent him spinning like a top out of the course. Unfortunately, Miss Michael was knocked in the opposite direction into the path of the horses, most of which either struck her or passed over her. A Doctor who was also standing nearby gave her assistance, but it was apparent that she had received very serious head injuries and was pronounced dead shortly afterwards.

At the inquest, Mr T.C Beaumont acting on behalf of the Beverley Race Company, explained that the

Company engaged about sixty police officers for the purpose of guarding the course. A verdict of accidental death was returned by the jury, who added a rider recommending more protection be given to the public at the point where the accident had occurred. Constable Kirby was commended for his plucky attempt to save the deceased. He was later awarded the sum of £5 out of public funds.

On the 29th May 1946 a staggering attendance was recorded of some 27.943 racegoer's, a figure unlikely to ever be beaten.

In 1957 an interesting visitor at the May meeting was former trainer Mr R.P. Botterill an eighty seven year old, who was born at Brough in the East Riding of Yorkshire, He originally commenced training at Doncaster before moving to Norton House, in Malton and turned out many winners. However at the outbreak of the second World War, the military authorities commandeered his stables.

On the 8th of June 1961, history was made at the track when the prize money for one race reached a four figure sum for the first ever time when the field of six runners raced for £1,000 in the Red Cap Rose Bowl Handicap. The race was won by *Fusion* ridden by Jimmy Etherington and trained by R. Peacock the 5-2 favourite, beating the Pat Taylor's popular locally trained veteran, *Penitent.*

Lester Piggott first rode at Beverley at the two day August meeting in 1962, he had seven mounts during the two days and ended up winning on four of them. Two of the winners were for the Newmarket trainer Fred Armstrong.

Lester Piggott riding Petite Marmite to an easy victory in the Moors and Robson Red Cap Rose Bowl at Beverley in August 1966.

One incident that hit the headlines both on the television news and the national press, occurred on the 14th September 1994. Stuart Webster the Keighley born jockey was dragged from his mount, *Sailormaite*, by the Irish born jockey Kieran Fallon. The incident occurred just after the winning post and afterwards the two riders continued their disagreement in the confines of the weighing room and the jockeys changing room. As a result of this second altercation Webster received a broken nose. At the later convened disciplinary meeting of the Jockey Club, Fallon was found guilty of violent and improper conduct on a racecourse. He was suspended for six months, which at that time, was one of the stiffest sentences handed out by the Disciplinary Committee.

TRAVEL TIME

An example of the way horses arrived at race in days gone by, before the railways or any road transport to aid them, is clearly described by George Smelt. In 1832, George left his job at the Rose and Crown Inn at Beverley to take up a position at the stable of Len Heseltine at Hambleton, a position he obtained, with the help and recommendation of racehorse owner Mr J Hopkinson of Bullings Hill, near Hornsea on the East Coast of Yorkshire. To get to the stable young George left Beverley on the 7a.m Trafalgar coach and travelled to York. He then walked from York to Easingwold and there stayed in overnight accommodation. The following morning he set off on foot to Hambleton, as he neared his destination he saw the wide expanse of the countryside and feeling isolated and lonely he sat on the roadside and cried. However, young George was determined and continued his journey and he eventually arrived at Mr Heseltine's stables. At first he was rather subdued and down in the dumps, but quite quickly he settled in to the routine, found some good work mates and was kept very busy.

He was soon given the task of taking 'his' horse *Inheritor* to the races and as a fourteen year old, it was no mean feat to get him and the horse to Manchester racecourse. The horse came in second, so then he would have to re-trace his journey back to Hambleton. His next outing was to take a two year old to Stockton Races called *Wyndham*, who won his race. Smelt later described these types of journeys. He and the horse would travel between eighteen and twenty-five miles a day, according to the weather. Arrangements were made ahead for their accommodation. Some trainers insisted upon the horse being led all the way, others preferred them to be ridden occasionally for a few miles, so that they might reduce the time on the road. At other times they were instructed to ride at a faster pace, this would ensure the lads arrived at their destination in a less tired condition.

The expenses for the horse and lad averaged ten shillings and sixpence a day on the road, this included staying the night at an Inn. The expenses of a trainer or head lad, with a hack, were from twelve shillings to fifteen shillings a day. No travelling expenses were allowed the lads, however they were given a half a crown for pocket money, the trainer was responsible for 'squaring-up' at the posting houses used for overnight stays. As a rule the lad slept with or near the horses.

It normally took three days from Hambleton to reach the racecourses at Newcastle or Doncaster, and four days to Manchester, so that the final gallops had to be given a week or so before the race in which the horse was entered.

RICHARD WATT

Richard Watt purchased the Bishop Burton estate in 1782, Richard was a Liverpool merchant who had acquired a vast fortune as a sugar planter and trader in Jamaica. On his death the estate was passed to his nephew and in turn to his son Richard, who took advantage of the wonderful facilities and he became one of the Country's leading racehorse breeders and trainers. He first registered his famous harlequin jacket in 1806.

The Hall was eventually purchased by Mr O.S. Hellyer who in 1951 sold the Hall and one farm to the county council. The Hall was demolished and a new building erected on the site, which in 1954 was opened as an agricultural college for 12 female and 28 male students. Today the college offers many varied course subjects and has accommodation for 225 students.

In 1876, a race that is still run today appeared on the race card, The Watt Memorial Plate. The race was set up after the death of 'Squire' Richard Watt. The 'Squire' was born in 1786 and was the grand-nephew of a sailor turned West-Indies plantation owner, and was a very wealthy man who resided in Bishop Burton near Beverley in a large house which was surrounded by lots of land which he used for training and breeding race horses. He owned the winner of the 1813 St Leger, a horse with a very familiar name, *Altisidora.* This famous win induced Mr Watt to re-name the village pub The Altisidora, so the public house had it's third name as it was originally named the Horse and Jockey and then the Evander before gaining the new name in 1813. The pub which remains known as the Altisidora in the village of Bishop Burton to this day. The "Squire" went onto win another three St Leger's, with *Barefoot* in 1823, *Mennon* in 1825 and *Rockingham* in 1833. Incidentally, another pub took the latter's name, The Rockingham Arms at Lockington (sadly now closed) a village which lies between Beverley and Driffield and which was once owned by the Hotham family and for many years only had a six day licence and never opened on the Sabbath.

Another horse to win the Watt Memorial Plate was *Tommy Tittlemouse*, who won 40 races in all. And was trained by J.T. Whipp at Mount Pleasant on the Bishop Burton side of Beverley. *Tommy Tittlemouse* had the distinction of being the final ride of one of the finest jockeys this Country has ever seen, the one and only Fred Archer, the date was the 4th November 1886 at the now defunct racecourse at Lewes.

Fred rode his first winner at the age of 13 years, and during his far too brief career, rode 2.748 winners from 8.004 mounts, within this total, Fred rode 21 classic winners including 5 Derby's. He was born on the 11th of January 1857 and on the 8th of November 1886 at the age of 29 years he took up his revolver and shot himself dead in the presence of his sister.

At the time of his death, Doctors were treating him for a fever, later diagnosed as typhoid. For years he had struggled with his weight and many blamed the years of wasting that had caused his illness and depression.

A great friend of Archer's who was one of the great gambler's of the time, who not only bought horses, but also prepared or trained them. What is more he was East Yorkshire born and bred, his name, Captain James Octavious Machell. James was born at Etton Rectory near Beverley on the 5th December 1837 the youngest child of the Reverend Robert and Eliza Machell. When old enough, he decided to make a career in the Army, however he loved the 'Sport of Kings', and at the age of 25 he resigned his Commission because he had been refused leave to attend a race meeting at Doncaster.

In 1880 he was named as a Steward at Beverley races at the meeting of June 2nd, together with The Duke of Montrose, Viscount Helmsley (who tragically died in Madeira the following year aged just 29) Christopher Sykes (son of Sir Tatton Sykes of Sledmere) Colonel WHH Broadley (who for many years was the M.P for the East Riding) Alfred Crosskill (son of William Crosskill, manufactory, of farm machinery etc) and others.

One of his great training feats, was after he identified a future Derby winner at the annual yearling sales at Ealtham. At the sales, he accompanied Henry Chaplin, acting as his Racing Manager. When Lot 27 came under the hammer, a classy, well bred individual, created a lot of interest particular to Captain Machell and the Marquis of Hastings. The bidding quickly rose by fifty guineas at a time and in the end, Chaplin after a brief conversation with the Captain, called. "One thousand guineas" and secured the nameless colt.

The colt was eventually given the name *Hermit* and as a two year old was being briefly trained at Findon by William Goater for which he won four of his six races. However he commenced his 3 year old career in the hands of George Bloss, with of course, assistance from the Captain. So. In 1867, the colt was entered for that years Derby, a race he would win and foiled a gamble that the Marquis of Hastings had planned. So the Marquis was thwarted for a second time by the Captain. Apart from the Derby the Captain won two Grand Nationals, and it was reported that he won enough money to buy back an Estate in Westmorland that was in the ownership of his family some 50 years before.

Another twist in the 1867 Derby, saw Machell take bets from the Duke of Hamilton, the Duke could be described, as the original 'mug punter'. He was so convinced that the *Hermit* would not win the Derby that he offered Captain Machell 30.000 to 1, not once but six times prior to the day of the race, each time the Captain matched the offer with a £1.000, so that the Duke stood to lose £180.000.

On the eve of the race the Duke pleaded with the Captain to have the bets called off, and fortunately for the Duke, the Captain agreed.

Over the years the Captain suffered from depression and spells of gout. The Captain remained unmarried and died in 1902 at 65 years of age, he was buried in the same cemetery in Newmarket as Fred Archer, they were great friends for many years, that is until the Captain thought that Fred had given him some false information in one particular race. The Captain took Fred's death badly and never forgave himself for snubbing his friend for so many years.

EAST RIDING PARSONS

Whilst Captain Machell was only the son of a Parson, it was not unusual for Parsons to be involved in horse racing, particularly in the early to mid 1800's. The East Riding of Yorkshire had a number of fine Parson/Jockeys, one in particular had the reputation of being one of the finest cross-country riders in England. His name was the Reverend John Bower. Reverend Bower hailed from Bridlington on the east coast, and had gained the reputation of being the best and hardest rider in the three Riding's. In those days horse racing was quite often run in heats, Sir Tatton Sykes rode one of his own horse's in a Hunters Stake at Catterick Bridge, and was beaten in the first heat, mainly due to the fact that he was really tired after riding from Morpeth races, he had travelled on horseback throughout the night to race at Catterick, as a result he had not slept at all. He realised he would not be at his best and that he should not have been beaten in the first heat. With that in mind, he approached the Reverend Bower, and asked him to take the ride in the second heat, so into the famous orange jacket the vicar was only to pleased to wear. He went on to win the second and third heats quite easily. Another Parson who became a regular visitor to the stable at Malton of John Scott was the Reverend Edward Trueman who was based at nearby North Grimston.

PUBLIC ORDER

The headlines in the Beverley Guardian on the 21st of June 1924 was as follows:- Racecourse Pests at Beverley- Card Sharpers and 'Welshers' convicted. A report revealed that a special police court was held on the evening of the first days race meeting. A total of five people appeared at the Magistrates Court, four of them were charged with gaming for playing "Spinning Jenny" and the three card trick and were all fined £5. The fifth man a Harry Carling, was charged with stealing by welshing eight shillings from three racegoer's. Carling was acting as a bookmaker on the racecourse, and was laying a point better odds than other bookmakers on a filly named *Lady Bayardo* who was favourite to win the 4-15pm race. Just as the filly passed the winning post, detectives saw Carling and his Clerk run off in different directions, unfortunately for Carling he was the one caught by the police. In court the Magistrate's were told that he had previous convictions for uttering (passing) counterfeit coins at Birmingham and for loitering at Doncaster. He was committed for 3 months with hard labour and ordered to pay restitution out of the £10-17shillings that was found in his possession at the time of his arrest.

The following day, many of the racing public were brought before the Magistrate's, mainly for drunk and disorderly offences. One particular young married man from nearby Hull found his way to the Cottage Hospital in Morton Lane, Beverley to have an injury to his head treated. He was very drunk and obstreperous, and one of the Doctors on duty gave him an injection in an attempt to quieten him down, he was then ejected from the hospital and was arrested by the police in Morton Lane.

The report on the races was somewhat downbeat,

the weather was glorious but the poor attendance was attributed to the unemployment situation and scarcity of money.

A BEVERLEY CUSTOM BEFORE RACING

In the mid 1800's when horse racing at Beverley was enjoying more success than neighbouring York races who had entered a period of decline, due mainly to the obstructive nature of the Knavesmire pasture master's. Another custom was literally played out in the streets of Beverley on the Sunday of race-week. This was when a hell raising game of football took place between two teams described as the 'loose' men of Beverley and the surrounding villages. The game kicked off at the race-course and continued through the centre of Beverley. Beverley were generally superior, but one year the lads from the villages had their opponents under severe pressure, until a certain Bob Spence, a local butcher rescued the local team with a tremendous kick from the Rose & Crown, it cleared the North Bar, and both teams set off in hot pursuit. Meanwhile, in the nearby church, presumable St Mary's, all was peace and tranquillity as the strains of the organ accompanied the dignified exit of many local dignitaries. They were not best pleased when the Mayor of Beverley was knocked to the ground by this gang of marauding local footballers. And whilst no one was hurt, the Mayor a Mr Williams and his fellow Councillors swore revenge.

A plan was hatched the following year and Ruddock the bellman, emerged from a hiding place, scooped up the ball and made for a thorn hedge, behind which a horse was ready to convey him and his prize swiftly away. Poor Ruddock however, clearly lacked a turn of foot, and a hand grabbed his ankle before he could clamber over the hedge. Gallantly he managed to pass the ball to a Constable on the other side. Ruddock, unfortunately was practically disembowelled for his pains by the outraged footballers. They dragged him fifty yards along the top of the hedge. The poor Constable fared little better, for as the ball arrived at his hands, a large piece of rock thrown from the crowd struck him on the head and he fell down unconscious. With the ball retrieved, the game resumed. The offenders were rounded up in due course, and they were brought before the Magistrates, before being confined to hard labour.

The following year when the players gathered as usual to play the game, the Mayor appeared at the head of 40 militia, he read out the Riot Act and was met with moans and jeers from the assembled teams, however with a charge of fixed bayonets, they were soon quickly silenced and dispersed. So in 1825 the traditional game of football, was ended once and for all

POLICING BEVERLEY RACE DAY

When Beverley held single day race meetings, the population of the town grew enormously and the local police were supplemented by Officers from neighbouring Forces. These were housed for the day in spare rooms at one of Beverley's oldest public houses, The Beaver in North Bar Within, The Beaver had at least two other names before it's present one, having previously been known as The Wheatsheaf before taking the name, The George, in 1850. The landlord was advised and always ensured that the bars had no moveable furniture in them, and the police always patrolled the streets of Beverley in pairs, looking for troublemakers.

At the May meetings of 1946 record crowds attended the two day meetings, it was also the first occasion that the East Riding Police had been solely responsible for policing the town and the races. A Special Court was arranged for any transgressors, one of the first to be led into the Dock was a certain Charles Hamblett of Barlby, near Doncaster. He was arrested at the races and pleaded guilty to playing the three card trick. He was fined £5.

With the second world war not long ended, it was not surprising to see that the two day meeting attracted fifteen thousand spectators on the first day and despite a wet day ten thousand turned out for the second day

In June 1955 the Royal Ascot meeting had to be cancelled due to a rail strike taking place. That meant the only meeting to take place in England at that time was at Beverley on the 15th and 16th of June. Many of the top jockeys of that era travelled north to Beverley including the Champion Jockey at that time Dougie Smith, he had a mount in every race but only rode one winner that was on the 4-9 favourite *Sikander.* Other top jockeys included the Royal jockey WH Carr who rode *Bay Comet* to win and E. (Manny) Mercer the brother of Joe who rode the final winner on *Light Mist* at odds of 7-4. Incidentally four years later Manny was tragically killed when being thrown from *Priddy Fair* whilst going down to the start in a race at Ascot.

STARTING GATES

For the June 19th and 20th meeting in 1900 the Directors of Beverley racecourse decided to install a new innovation for the start of two year old races. It was the Gray's "starting gate", it was trialled at considerable expense in the hope that it would not only improve starts but encourage owners to enter their horses and give punters more confidence, in that their fancy would not be left at the start, particularly in the five furlong events. The starting barrier was pioneered in Australia by Alexander Gray who was later helped by his son Reuben, who as a jockey had been fined £5 for allowing his mount to step over a white chalk mark. Which was used at the start of races.

By the 1920's the single strand barrier designed by the Gray's, was replaced by a spring-powered five-strand device, designed by Johnstone and Gleeson. A system that was gradually replaced by the use of starting stalls by the Jockey Club from 1965.

The racecourse at Beverley, like many others, was closed during the First World War and used as an airfield, with racing resuming in 1920. The course was again in military occupation during the Second World War, and the traditional two day meeting was revived in 1946.

It is interesting to learn that the 'tan gallop' on the Westwood was made about 1870 and was still used for the training of horses in 1988, and can still be seen to this day.

One of the sights often seen at any racecourse or Market square, was of the tipster, he was dressed

No free tips here

to look the part either in riding breeches or very well turned out and looking as prosperous as they come. Also, it was mandatory to carry an expensive looking pair of binoculars. They always attracted a large crowd, and they knew everyone in racing, they were on first name terms with all the leading trainers and jockeys. No one could resist spending a shilling (five new pence) for the brown envelope which contained at least three winners (allegedly) for the days meeting. But these characters could keep you spell bound just with their fantastic racing knowledge. Saturday Market, Beverley was certainly the place to be, prior to the days racing. However, near Beckside, Beverley, another tipster whom visitors to the town looked forward to seeing, and as an added bonus, his tips were free, were those displayed by a local cobbler in his shop window. On the morning of the races he would chalk them onto a large piece of leather, it was assumed that he had picked up some useful local information, as many people swore by his tips.

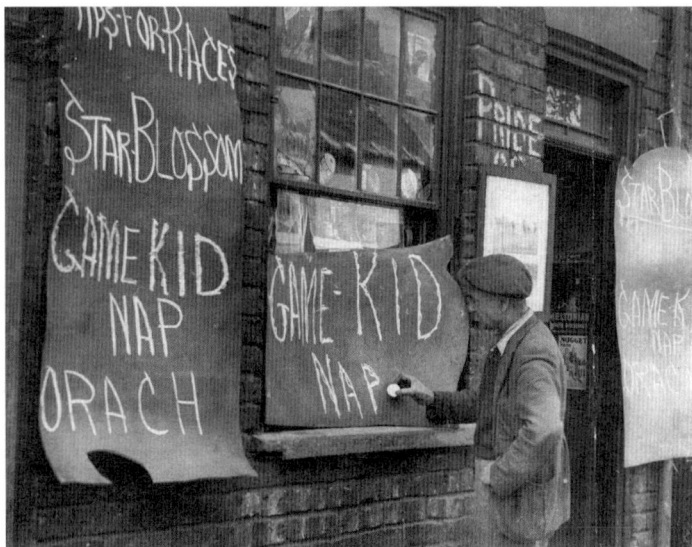

Free tips for Beverley Racegoers

One of the race-goer's from Hull, who loved his racing, and eventually became a well known betting shop manager for one of the leading bookmaker's was Ron Grantham. Ron later published a book with some great poems about his life, family and life in general. One of the poems was about a meeting with one of these tipsters, when he visited Beverley Races, the poem went as follows,

A TIPSTERS LESSON

I met a tipster on the Beverley course,

Who suggested that I back his horse.

A bonny filly, I agreed,

Stout hearted and well pedigreed.

His asking was the smallest fee

For the guaranteed winner of the half past three.

The time soon came for the filly to run,

I'd gambled my shirt-oh what had I done.

The flag was raised at the starters call,

With the crash of the gates they flew from the stall.

The event was run at a hell of a pace

And the whips flew high in the three thirty race.

Voices in chorus deafened the ear,

The favourite was last and the bookies did cheer.

The filly I backed was favourite of course,

I left dear old Beverley full of remorse.

That tipster taught me when your luck it desserts,

To lose all your cash is painful and hurts.

But the biggest of fools with pneumonia flirts,

When they lose all their cash as well as their shirts.

Work in progress on the new members stand (1958).

OPENING OF MEMBERS GRANDSTAND

On May 9th 1959 Lord Irwin who at that time was Senior Steward of the Jockey Club, attended Beverley opening fixture to officially open the new stabling area, a new much larger paddock area. But the main purpose of his visit was to open the new Members Grandstand which had been built at a cost of £35.000. This new facility gave the Members an increased seating area and replaced the old Jubilee stand which was built as long ago as 1887. Members at that time were paying £6 for an annual badge for 6 days racing, a race card and car parking facility was included.

Work is comlete on the new members stand (1959)

BEVERLEY SPONSORS

Beverley have always been to the forefront of Sponsorship deals and the present Chief Executive Sally Iggulden and the Chairman Charles Maxstead are keen to encourage new and old sponsors to the racecourse. This photograph shows a young looking Michael Stoute receiving his trophy over 42 years ago from sponsors that are still with Beverley to this day. A remarkable achievement.

Michael Stoute recieving The Hovingham Trophy from Mis Vanessa Needler after his Lord Aquarius won the sponsors race at Beverley in July 1974. (Left to Right) Sidney Renton Managing Director of Beverley Race Company, Harold Needler of the sponsors, Gil Cullingham Chairman of Beverley Race Company and Christopher Needler.

LIGHTWEIGHT JOCKEYS

It is unusual to find many jockeys weighing less than 7stone 7 pounds in the modern day racing, unless of course you are a young apprentice. However in days gone by when young apprentices could be riding whist still at school, it was not unusual for them to weigh less than four stone. An example of this, was the Classic winning jockey George Fordham, he rode his first winner in 1851 at the age of 14 years of age and two years later he rode the winner of the Cambridgeshire Handicap on *Little David* at that time he was reputed to weigh 3 stone 12 pounds. Later a lad named James Adams, he was born in 1863 at Nunnington, North Yorkshire was riding race horses in their work from the age of nine. At the age of fourteen he won a hurdle race .

One of the original great jockeys to be born in the East Riding was Leonard Jewison. He was the son of a Beverley butcher, Leonard was a tall, slim gawky young man, and never let his impediment of only having one eye, stop him in his quest for riding winners.

Another Beverley man who rode three St Leger winners, was Job Marson junior, he was the son of the trainer responsible for training one of the great locally owned race horses. The mare *Nancy*, was the racehorse that saw some remarkable scenes in Beverley. She was bred by Mr C Baxter, in the East Riding at Burton Pidsea, where the name of the village Inn was changed to ensure that her name and fame would be forever remembered. Job senior, once a leading jockey himself trained the mare, and when she won the Chester Cup, most folks in Beverley knew she was partly owned by the Reverend Jennings of Watton, a tiny hamlet between Driffield and Beverley.

In 1851, *Nancy,* competed in thirteen races, and she was only beaten on one occasion. Including winning the Chester Cup, carrying the weight of only four stone and twelve pounds, when she beat the mighty *Voltigeur* by a length, who was giving 33 lbs to the winner. It is reported that when *Nancy* returned to Beverley (where the locals between them won a small fortune) most of the inhabitants turned out to wait for her at the railway station. Even the Beverley Town band played as the mare ridden by Frank Marson proceeded through the town to the home of Tom Lister (another to have a share in her). After the brief visit, the mare and crowd continued the journey through the town to her stable near the Rose & Crown. Unfortunately for *Nancy*, whilst competing in another race at Chester, she was killed after breaking a leg.

Two years earlier, an even bigger event took Beverley into the sporting newspapers and for that matter most of the other national periodicals. In 1849 *Peter Simple* trained by T Cunningham and ridden by him, won the first of his two Grand National victories. *Peter Simple* was owned by Finch Mason Junior. The story of the race was one of grief for the majority of the runners, in fact only two of the runners were left in the race with any chance of winning some three-quarters of a mile from the finish. Captain D'Arcy was on *The Knight of Gwynne* with Tom Cunningham riding *Peter Simple*. D'Arcy stood to win a fortune if he won the race, and the story goes, that he offered Tom two 'monkeys' (£1.000) to pull *Peter Simple*. Cunningham refused the offer, whereupon two fences later D'Arcy upped the offer to £4.000. But our Tom was not to be bribed, and *Peter Simple* won by three lengths at odds of 20-1, *The Knight of Gwynne* came in second place at odds of 8-1. Favourite that year was a horse named *Prince George* who took third place, beaten a distance at odds of 4-1.

Just before Tom won the National on *Peter Simple*, he was riding at Didcot and one of the biggest Bookmakers of the day, a man called Davis approached Tom on the railway platform and said, "I see you have a horse in the Grand National?" "I have", replied Tom. Davis said, "I will lay you 100-1, if you want a bet?" Tom quietly pulled out three £10 notes and said, "I'll take £3.000 to that". After the Grand National, Davis approached Tom and handed over thirty £100 notes, slapped Tom on the back and said, "Well done Thomas, you rode a good race and deserved to win".

Some years later, Tom's son Charles trained at Beverley and turned out many winners. He later accepted a lucrative position as a trainer in Buenos Ayres; he eventually returned to Beverley and retired. Another son, Tom junior, died in France where he had much success as a trainer.

Incidentally, when *Peter Simple* won his second Grand National in 1853 he had left Tom Cunningham, and was ridden and trained by Tom Oliver and owned by Josey Little. Oliver loved the good life and was always on the brink of bankruptcy, and for a time, spent a short time in prison. However before the 1853 Grand National he told the owner, "Sometimes he means it and I don't, sometimes I mean it, and he don't, but today we both mean it". His words rang true and *Peter Simple* won at the odds of 9-1 and in doing so, became the oldest horse at 15 years to ever win the Grand National, a record that still stands to this day.

Pocklington near York, also produced a great jockey named James ('Jim') Snowden. His parents were Hawkers and used to travel over the Yorkshire Wolds with a cart laden with pots, pans, brushes and the like. Jim served his apprenticeship with a Beverley farmer called J Pickering, Pickering also trained a few racehorses on the side at Nancy House. "Jim" weighed just four stone and In 1860 at the age of 17 years he rode *Butterfly* to win the Oaks at Epsom. *Butterfly* was trained by G Oates and owned by Richard Eastwood. After "Jim" had completed his apprenticeship, he moved to Richmond in North Yorkshire to live. He became first jockey to 'Squire' Watt of Bishop Burton near Beverley. In 1863 he was successful on Mr Gilby's horse *Jackal* which won the Scurry Stakes at Beverley at odds of 2-1. this was the Thursday of a two day meeting commencing the previous day. The local newspaper reported that the road leading up to the racecourse was well attended by the members of the swindling profession (mainly card sharps) and that the shooting galleries were well patronised and the proprietors of the gaming tables did an extensive business. The Beverley Cup the big race on the first day was won by *Borealis* a three year old at odds of 2-1.

Unfortunately 'Jim' enjoyed a drink or two, on one occasion he went to Chester to ride for the Duke of Westminster, when he arrived at his hotel, he remarked to the landlord, "Things are very quiet for the races tomorrow. Has no one turned up yet?". "Races!", replied the landlord "they were last week, and everyone was asking, where's Jim Snowden?". He had been on a bout of drinking and had forgotten all about Chester races. Needless to say, he never rode for the Duke of Westminster again.

'Jim' was once described by the leading Malton trainer, William I'anson, "as the greatest jockey, drunk or sober, I ever saw". Jim apparently was often in the former state. On one occasion at Catterick, when shown his mount in the parade ring, he said, "Tak them blinkers off- a blind hoss and a blind jockey will never dee". He died in poverty at Bentley near Doncaster on February 6th 1889 aged 45 years and lies beneath a memorial stone (subscribed to by his many racing friends) in the church yard at Pocklington.

One of East Yorkshire's most successful jockeys of all time was probable Sim Templeman, he served his apprenticeship with Sykes of Malton and had his first ride in public at the Malton course in 1819. He had to wait until 1821 before riding his first ever winner at Catterick.

In 1839 he won the Derby on a colt called *Bloomsbury* who started at the generous odds of 25-1. The race was run in a snow storm and it was a bitterly cold day, Sim rode a brilliant waiting race and only came to win the race in the last furlong, winning 'cleverly' by a length. In 1847 and 1848 he was successful in both the Oaks and the Derby. In 1851 he was on *Newminster* when he won the St Leger.

It was at Burnby, close to Pocklington that Sim died in 1884, he died in the very house that he had built after one of Derby wins.

Another jockey associated with the St Leger, who was born in the village of Pocklington, was John Cade he had the privilege of riding the second ever running of this great Classic.

Another East Yorkshire jockey to shine, was the Catwick born Frank Collinson. Frank and his brother were the sons of a farmer and both left home to take up apprenticeships with Christopher Jackson at Middleham. In 1808 Frank won the

Derby on Sir Hedworth Williamson', *Pan* at odds of 25-1. Unfortunately on his way to Epsom, Frank slept in a damp bed, which was thought to have brought on an illness which led to his death four years later at Ashgill, Middleham, where he had been training for two or three years.

Thomas Field was born in the village of Melbourne near Pocklington, and was a jockey of some repute, he rode many winners which included the 1799 St Leger, before taking up training at Richmond, North Yorkshire.

Tommy Weldon was also a Yorkshire born jockey who rode with great distinction. After his retirement from the saddle, he settled in Beverley but spent most of his time at the nearby village of Bishop Burton. Finding time on his hands, he tried his hand at training even to the extent of purchasing 'Tupgill' Stables at Middleham, however a short time later he sold them to R.W. Armstrong. To be fair to Tommy, he never really recovered from an accident that occurred during the running of the 1901 Oaks at Epsom, when his mount *Arta* and another runner *Marshcress* both fell. Tragically Tommy died at the early age of 46 years, whilst sitting in a chair at home. Just before his death Tommy had expressed the wish, that when the end came, his poor tired body might be laid to rest up on the hill in Bishop Burton's Kirkyard, where two or three generations of the famous Watts lay. His wish was granted, and quite near to the Hall-Watt vault is a marble cross bearing the following simple inscription:- <u>In ever loving memory of Thomas Weldon, Born November 2nd 1858, Died April 21st, 1905.</u>

Whilst many of the older racegoer, particular the Beverley supporter will recall the exploits of horses like Crusadors Horn, Penitent or Chebb's Lad there is one race horse that became a real favourite of both the young and old alike and he became a standing order at any Beverley meeting he ran at.

The horse was owned by a vetinary Surgeon, Steve Borsberry and his wife Pam, who were almost lost entirely to the world of horse racing. Earlier they owned two horses, and they only ran one race between them, one broke a leg the other broke it's back. Fortunately the couple decided to carry on and asked trainer John Spearing to purchase them a jumper who, at that time was based at Alcester, in Warwickshire. John did find them a horse, a three year old for the princely sum of 2.500 guineas at the Doncaster sales his name was Rapid Lad. He was only pony size but within a week had won a hurdle race at Ludlow. Shortly after his first success he won again in a similar race at Market Rasen . The handicapper soon put his weight up and because of his size or lack of it, he was returned to racing on the flat. He was immediately rewarded with a win at Brighton, however the following season he really showed his liking for Beverley racecourse by winning four races, this despite suffering from sore feet, tendon trouble and bad joints. He soon became a favourite with the crowd and just loved the place. Between the years 1983 and 1989 he won a total of twelve races, was second on six occasions and came in fourth on no less than five occasions. Rapid Lad now has a mile and a quarter Handicap Stakes named in his honour and is run annually. A large bar area is also named after him, not bad for a race horse that cost less than £3.000.

YORKSHIRE STUDS

SLEDMERE HOUSE

Sledmere a beautiful village not far from the Capital of the Wolds, Driffield, has been the home of generations of the Sykes family. Horses and in particular the breeding of them has always been part of the family's history.

Sir Christopher Sykes rebuilt Sledmere House in 1780 but it was destroyed by fire in 1911, and again rebuilt. Sir Christopher died in 1801 and was succeeded by his son, Mark Masterman Sykes who was born in 1771, Mark was a great sportsman. In 1804 he began to race horses on a small scale, he ran a horse in that year's St Leger, and won a Sweepstake with *Sir Pertinox,* which Mr Tatton Sykes rode for him. In the same year, Sir Mark began to hunt, later Tatton Sykes managed his brother's hounds, which up to 1816 hunted to the walls of York City.

In 1820 he practically retired from public life, owing to ill-health, and whilst on his way down south died at Weymouth on the 16th February 1823 aged 52 years.

Then came the era of Sir Tatton Sykes, and for a couple of years, he continued to live at Westow. He loved riding and rode well into his sixties, on one occasion after riding the 63 miles from Sledmere one morning, he came second in the Macaroni

Stakes at Pontefract, he slept at Doncaster that night, and was beaten in another four-mile heat race at Lincoln the very next day.

Before Sir Tatton went to live at Sledmere in 1826, Mr Christopher Sykes had bred some bloodstock there and Sir Mark owned *Whitelock*, sire of *Blacklock*. It was, however the first Sir Tatton who laid the foundation of the Sledmere Stud. Sir Tatton's father believed in quantity, his son however was all for quality. Later the Stud was much reduced, however in 1865 the mare *Miss Agnes* gave birth to a filly foal by *The Cure*, she was so small and weedy that Sir Tatton told his stud groom, to put her down or give her away. The groom, James Snarry, kept her for himself, and so began one of the romances of the turf at that time, for whilst *Miss* Agnes founded a family. It was In fact, her daughter, the unwanted *Lily Agnes who* was the keystone of the stud founded at Eaton Hall by the Duke of Westminster. However before her stud duties, James was delighted to see his weedy filly win a number of races. As a two year she won six races from six runs and following this great start to her career she followed this up by winning a further fifteen races including the Doncaster Cup and Ebor Handicap. She, of course, was the dam of the mighty *Ormonde-* the 1886 Triple Crown winner- and later *Orme* who was trained by the great John Porter. He won the Middle Park and Dewhurst Stakes as a 2 year old and went onto win two Eclipse Stakes as a 3 and 4 year old. And remained unbeaten throughout his career.

Sir Tatton Sykes who gave his name to the 1846 St Leger winner, witnessed seventy six (76) St Leger winners in his ninety one years, this fact must rate Sir Tatton as Doncaster's best supporter of all time.

In August 1954, Her Majesty the Queen arrived by air at the Royal Air Force Station, Driffield from Scotland, for a three day visit to stay with Sir Richard and Lady Sykes at Sledmere. She spent considerable time looking round the famous Sledmere Stud and also took time to travel to the nearby equally famous Burton Agnes Stud, before flying back to Scotland.

RISE PARK

Rise not that far from Beverley and Hull has always been to the forefront of racing and racehorses. One of the earliest horses in the General Stud Book is *Ruffler*, foaled just before the year 1700 and was bred by Mr Hugh Bethell of Rise Park. This horse won a number of races, one of which was at Bramham Moor, for which Hugh received a gold cup that had been donated by Queen Anne. This trophy was eventually sent to auction in 1929, and reached a final bid of £5.000.

It was the late Captain Adrian Bethell who died in 1941, who revived the family interest in the Turf, and had a few horses with Captain Elsey at Malton. In addition he was Joint - Master with another Turfite, Major W Newland Hillas, of the Holderness Hounds. Captain Bethell was a fine horseman, an officer in the Life Guards; he was keenly interested in both bloodstock and hounds. Both have been bred and kept at Rise Park from time immemorial. It was custom to train the Bethell racehorse in Rise Park up to a certain point, and then send them to Malton to be given their final gallops for forthcoming events.

The Bethell family have been at the fore-front of breeding, racing and training racehorses, and clearly remain so today. Indeed the family have been connected with the Turf for over 300 years and in 1977 Mr R. A. (Tony) Bethell was elected a full member of the Jockey Club. He had acted as a Steward at Beverley races for several years and had also carried on the family tradition of training a string of National Hunt horses under the conditions of a Permit.

BURTON AGNES STUD

Burton Agnes Hall, dates back to the year 1173, when Roger de Stuteville built the Norman manor house, the lower chamber of which still remains to this day. The house has never changed hands by sale, although it has it has been in the custody of various families when the male line has ended

The Burton Agnes Stud, is situated a mile south of Burton Agnes Hall in the village of Burton Agnes which lies between Driffield and Bridlington was founded by Captain T.L Wickham-Boynton whose death in 1942 was a great loss, not only to the world of bloodstock, but in particular to the East Riding of Yorkshire. The Captain was not even a Yorkshire man, having originated from Boston Spa. He was educated at Eton and arrived at Burton Agnes in 1889. He soon set up the Stud, with the arrival of a number of stallions. His first stallion was named *Not Out* which he owned in partnership with Sir Tatton Syke's cousin and

Stud Manager, Mr Henry Cholmondeley, this particular stallion was later sold to the Hungarian Government, In those days the Captain went for stallions able to provide good hunters. However this strategy was changed to providing first class racing sires, this proved a popular move and well over sixty visiting mares enjoyed the five hundred acres of grass land at Burton Agnes Stud. When the Captain passed away, his wife took over the running of the Estate until her death in 1947. She was succeeded by her son Marcus and he decided a better option, would be to produce commercial yearlings, and from that time built up an enviable broodmare band.

The stud closed in 2009 and now provides first class facilities for boarding mares, sales preparation, rest and recuperation of horses in/out of training of racehorses and others, and the breaking of yearlings for owners and trainers.

THOROUGHBRED STUD

Cottingham is reported to be the largest village in England and is not far from the town of Kingston upon Hull. The village of Cottingham is not a place you would associate with the breeding of an Epsom Derby winner. The stud was founded by Crowther Harrison however in 1884 he handed over the management of the stud to his son John Simons Harrison, and it was John who was responsible for the breeding of the 1887 Epsom Derby winner, *Merry Hampton* at the price of 100-9 and ridden by John Watts, (who incidentally was the great -grandfather to John William "Bill" Watts who trained *Waterloo* to win the 1972 1000 guineas and *Teleprompter* to win the

Arlington Million in 1985).

Merry Hampton, was originally sent to the Doncaster sales and was bought by Mr 'Abington' Baird for 3.100 guineas. His first ever race was in the Derby, which he won by four lengths, and he never won another race, although he did come second in the St Leger.

John kept the stud going for 50 years and during his life attended 60 St Legers and was in great demand as a judge of thoroughbred stallions and exported many of best stock abroad, the best of which was thought to be *Comedy King* the winner of the 1910 Melbourne Cup. John eventually gave up the stud and his son Raymond Simons Harrison continued the long family association with bloodstock, being commissioned to buy at the Doncaster and Newmarket sales. Unfortunately he died at an early age in 1942, when dying suddenly at Beverley at the age of 57 years.

THE CARNABY STUD

The Carnaby Stud was apparently established by George Robinson about the year 1827, two years later he had a winner at Beverley when *Bolivov* won a Sweepstake and later the Doncaster Cup. However it was *Melbourne* who really put the stud on the map. One day a certain Mr Sidney Herbert visited the stud and saw three yearlings, he purchased two of them at 250 guineas apiece, but said of Melbourne, he had two bad knees, and offered less money, to which Henry Robinson (Georges son) refused point blank. Henry tried to train *Melbourne* himself, before sending the colt to Job Marston at Beverley, and later to Len Hesseltine at Hambleton. In 1835 *Melbourne* won the Gold Cup at Lincoln and a handicap at York. In 1839 further success came at Beverley, York, Nottingham and other minor courses. In 1842 he went to stud, standing first at the Rose and Crown at Beverley, at the modest fee of ten guineas.

Later, Lord George Bentinck, leased the stallion for a whole covering season for just £250, as a result he sired a number of winners, including *West Australian* who became the first winner of The 'Triple Crown'.

GARROWBY STUD

Garrowby Stud, is situated, literally on the Yorkshire Wolds where the Vale of York gives way to the chalk based downland. Lord and Lady Halifax maintain a group of broodmares on the 100 acre Stud. The land is also used by other livestock for grazing.

The Stud will be forever be associated with the 1978 Derby winner *Shirley Heights*, a bay colt sired by Mill Reef. *Shirley Heights* was bred by the 2nd Earl of Halifax and his son Lord Irwin, but was reared at Lady Halifax's Swynford Paddock Stud, before making his way back to Yorkshire.

When *Shirley Heights* won the Derby, he certainly did it the hard way, he had about thirteen rivals ahead of him rounding Tattenham Corner, and did not really act on the downhill part of the track. His jockey Greville Starkey didn't panic and switched his willing mount towards an opening on the inside, and beat *Hawaiian Sound* at the winning post.

COPGROVE HALL STUD

Was originally founded by the owner/breeder Lionel Holliday and the Hall was his main residence. In 1969 the whole Estate was placed on the market, and included 1.619 acres, a seven bedroom house, 19 cottages a number of loose boxes plus 14 railed paddocks. A guide price of £400.000 was expected to be raised, however the estate was split up and Mr Guy Reed purchased the house and 50 acres of grass land surrounding the house. Mr Reed who made his fortune by spotting the potential of the frozen chicken and formed the Company Buxted Chickens. Mr Reed having previously occupied the stud at Nidd Hall, was to eventually move all his stock to Copgrove. His world famous racing colours of gold and black check, with pink sleeves and cap were so easily recognised, particularly on the racecourses in the north of England.

He had many smart horses, including the likes of *Warpath, Dakota, Shotgun* and *Tiddlewinks*. It was *La Gucaracha* that became his first Group One winner in 2005 when winning the Nunthorpe Stakes at York. However the one that gave him his best racing moment was *Shotgun*, who finished fourth to the great *Shergar* in the Derby, *Shotgun* was trained by Chris Thornton and ridden by Lester Piggott. Mr Reed's Secretary of some thirty odd years was Liz Hall the daughter of Sam, it was Liz who announced that Mr Reed had passed away in July 2013 aged 91 years.

CLIFF STUD

Cliff Stud is situated high above the small town

of Helmsley. The stud was originally known as the Helmsley Stud and was founded by William Thorpe, with the help of his trainer Mathew Peacock. Mr Thorpe died in 1946 and the following year the property was taken over by Noel Murless, who had started training just up the road at the top of Sutton Bank at Hambleton Lodge (where Kevin Ryan trains now) before moving to Hambleton House (where Bryan Smart trains now). Murless then moved to Bechampton (where he was the Champion trainer in his first season) and then onto Warren Place, where Sir Henry Cecil trained. In 1982 Henry Cecil (before his knighthood) took over the lease of Cliff Stud with others, from Duncambe Park Estate and has remained at the 250 acre site ever since. It is worth recording, that the late Sir Henry trained his first ever winner in Yorkshire. It was at Ripon on the 17th May, 1969, when *Celestial Cloud was* ridden to victory by Bill O'Gorman.

OUBOROUGH STUD

James Voase Rank was born in Kingston upon Hull in 1881, he was the eldest son of Joseph Rank the well known Miller. James was educated locally at Hymers College and eventually became the managing director of the family firm.

In 1934 he surprised some of his family by buying a stud farm near Salisbury, which was named "Ouborough" which he named after the name of the residence of the birth place of his mother Emily, in the village of Skirlaugh, in the East Riding of Yorkshire. James gained a reputation as one of the leading owners in the horse racing world and in 1938 won the St Leger with *Scottish Union*, ridden by Brownie Carslake and trained by Noel Cannon at the famous Druid's Lodge Stables on Salisbury Plain. And apart from breeding race horses he also became the breeder of Jersey cows and was one of the foremost breeders of, Great Danes, Irish Wolfhounds and Greyhounds. In 1931 his Greyhound 'Deeside' won the blue-ribbon of the Irish coursing season, the Irish Cup. James died in 1952, and the following year his home bred Great Dane, 'Elch Elder' of Ouborough won the Best in Show at Crufts.

HUNSLEY HOUSE STUD

Mr E. Vernon Stephenson of Hunsley House Stud, near Little Weighton not far from Beverley, was another gentleman who added to Easy Yorkshire's reputation as a nursery for bloodstock. Mr Stephenson was a keen hunting man, amateur trainer and rider, who combined farming with his love of horses. Vernon had the distinction of riding in the Grand National on two occasions, and on one particular mount, has served many a quizmaster well over the years. His mount *Derby Day* fell, which has prompted the horse racing question, "when did Derby Day fall on the day of the Grand National"? Over the years he had a few stallions, one of the most notable was *Atlas,* a horse that won the 1956 Doncaster Cup when ridden by Harry Carr and trained by Cecil Boyd -Rochfort and owned by the Queen. Unfortunately he was disappointing at stud.

Mr Stephenson passed away in 1974 and was succeeded by Mr R.S.A. Urquhart known to all as Bob. Bob was a former manager at the Whitsbury Stud, which was owned by probably the biggest and best known bookmaker in the world, the late William Hill at Fordingbridge, Hampshire.

In 1996 the former England skipper and then manager of Newcastle United Kevin Keegan, took time out from his football duties to visit his recently purchased stallion *Aragon* at the Hunsley House Stud and then went onto spend an afternoon at Beverley races, where he sponsored the 4.50 race, the Aragon Maiden Stakes. It was interesting to note that one of the runners was *Jonny's Joker*, which was owned and trained by ex-England International footballer Francis Lee. Kevin Keegan also owned another sixteen horses, which were trained by another former England International, Mick Channon.

Incidentally, *Aragon* succeeded the highly successful *Rambo Dancer* as the Hunsley House Stud stallion, who had moved into a new stud in Natel, in South Africa,

YAPHAM MILL STUD

Pocklington based Reg Bond enjoyed his horse racing from an early age, and was a frequent visitor to his local track, Beverley.

Several years later, this successful businessman has had the pleasure of welcoming his own horses into the winners enclosure. He has also owned horses that have won Group races and one of the most prestigious sprint handicaps of the season when *Bond Boy* ridden by Chris Catlin and trained in Yorkshire by Bryan Smart won the Stewards Cup at Goodwood at odds of 14-1. Reg owns Yapham Mill Stud which is located just north of Pocklington and adjoins his residence. Reg has been associated with many big race winners and one that stands out is the entire *Monsieur Bond,* who when his racing career ended stood at the Whitsbury Manor Stud before eventually returning to Yorkshire to stand at the Norton Grove Stud. Quite understandable Yapham Mill Stud have utilised this fine stallion on many occasions.

NORTON GROVE STUD

The Norton Grove Stud is situated in Norton, near Malton, North Yorkshire, was founded in the 1950's by Major Hudson who managed the stud until his death in 1995. The stud farm was then left to Major Hudson's stud groom, Richard Lingwood and his wife Maggie. The stud has gradually improved the quality of it's stallions over the past years and exiting times lie ahead for this go ahead family run stud farm. A leading stallion that has produced many Black type performers is *Monsieur Bond* other's include *Misu Bond* and *Milk it Mick.*

PARK FARM, RISE

Park Farm, Rise near Skirlaugh, Beverley East Yorkshire could never be described as a commercial stud. However many winners were bred there and ran in the colours of one of the East Riding's most enthusiastic of owners Mr Charles Buckton. In 1961 he owned a horse that caused a great surprise to everyone on the course, the name of the horse was *Big Time,* who, when ridden by Jimmy Etherington and trained by Mick Easterby won the Westwood Handicap at odds of 50-1 in a field of only 6 runners. However Mr Buckton loved the breeding aspect of racing, his best mare was undoubtedly, *My Old Dutch*, she was bought out of a seller for a few hundred guineas. Her most famous offspring was *Dutch Gold* who won over £20,000 in prize money and was one of the leading sprinters in the Country. However disaster struck when the mare was out grazing in one of the fields at the farm in July 1975, she was fatally struck down by lightning. In bloodstock circles she was worth thousands of pounds, but to Mr Buckton and his family she was priceless.

AIKE GRANGE STUD

Jill Banks formerly married to trainer Peter Ward, ran this Stud with her husband Stuart at this tiny Hamlet known to most local's as "Yak a'back of Arram" due to it's proximity to the other Hamlet just south of Aike pronounced 'Yak'. This quiet tiny village is serviced by a narrow road, with passing places, and not the sort of place you would envisage large horse boxes passing to and fro. But somehow John Sutcliffe the Epsom trainer managed to unload the first stallion to do duty at this very efficient stud, and that after dropping off his 1975 entry for the St Leger at Doncaster. The horse in question was the former 1972 Wokingham Stakes (Handicap)winner *Le Johnstan* who was the first of many stallions to begin their covering duties at this part of the East Riding. Others included, *Belfort, Kala Shikari, Dominion Royale, Dublin Taxi, Jimmy the Singer* and others. In 1987 it was *Le Johnston* who provided the winner of The Hull Daily Mail Handicap *Our Ginger* who was bought from Jill by trainer Ron

Thompson. The stud has now been converted to an International Dressage Centre.

MILLY and BERNARD SHAW

Just a few miles west of Jill Banks, Aike Grange Stud at nearby Lockington was the home of retired farmer Bernard Shaw and his wife Milly. The couple were known to me when they had farmed at nearby Willfholme. You would never have described their premises as a Stud Farm, but behind their detached bungalow were several acres of grass land. It was here that they raised some wonderful racehorses, Milly a horse enthusiast all her life and Bernard a great stockman who became a rather reluctant horse breeder. They bought two yearling fillies, one of which was named *She's Smart*, she had managed to win three races, and had been placed on ten other occasions, when trained by Peter Easterby. After she had finished racing Milly and Bernard decided to keep her as a brood mare, what a brilliant decision that was. She produced foals like *Rum Lad* who went on to win six races, *Smart Predator* who won twelve races and *Smart Hostess* the winner of seven of her races.

Milly and Bernard were at a stage in life that driving long distances was not on their agenda, so they rang me one day to ask if I fancied being their chauffer, I did not require asking twice and with a pal of mine Dave, took on the task of driving them to the races. *Rum Lad* had retired by that time so we joined them, when *Smart Predator* and *Smart Hostess* were in their prime. Both were trained by that brilliant Malton trainer John Quinn who was then based solely at Bellwood

Cottage Stables, Settrington near Malton, North Yorkshire. *Smart Predator* took us to places like, Goodwood, Epsom, Newmarket in the south of England and nearer home to York, Doncaster, Redcar, Haydock and many other race courses. One of his best races was when getting beat in a big sprint race at Epsom in 2001. He was ridden by Frankie Dettori and had a favoured stand side drawn stall 12 however those drawn 12, 13, 14 were at a disadvantage as the stalls opened late and John Reid riding the winner *Boleyn Castle* took the opportunity to grab the rail and was never headed. Giving the winner five pounds and a start was just beyond him and he finished a gallant second. One of the highlights for both Milly and Bernard must have been near the close of the 2003 flat season at Doncaster when John entered both *Smart Predator* and *Smart Hostess* in a race at Doncaster, *Smart Hostess* ridden by Robert Winston finished first beating *Smart Predator* ridden by Keith Dalgleish by the small margin of three quarters of a length. This result gave Mr and Mrs Shaw great satisfaction. Although earlier that year *Smart Predator* ridden by Keith Dalgleish may have given them as much pleasure when winning the first ever running of a race for grey horses only, held at Newmarket. This race is now run annually and very popular it is.

DONCASTER BLOODSTOCK SALES

Doncaster Bloodstock Sales was founded in 1962 by Willie Stephenson, the only Englishman to train a Derby winner and a Grand National winner, and Ken Oliver, a well known Scottish based auctioneer and National Hunt trainer.

However Bloodstock Sales have been part of the Doncaster horse racing scene for a very long time prior to 1962, In fact the St Leger Festival Yearling Sales are the oldest Bloodstock Sales in the United Kingdom.

Henry Beeby was the most recent Managing Director of Doncaster Bloodstock Sales; however in July 2006 they merged with Goff's to form a Bloodstock Auction House that aims to become Europe's leading Bloodstock Auctioneers with sales in Ireland, Doncaster and Kempton.

HOWDEN HORSE SALES

In 1807 the largest horse sale to be held in the whole of the Country was without doubt, held in the East Yorkshire village of Howden. It was attended by dealers from as far a field as London in the south and Edinburgh in the north and the large towns in between. It was estimated that over 4.000 horses were offered foe sale on a daily basis, and 16.000 horses were disposed of throughout the sale. Because of the popularity of the sale all the stables were completely full within a ten mile radius of Howden.

Sales were busy throughout the 1800's, and in 1874 it was reported that agents for the British and German Governments were prominent buyers for their respective cavalry's, these sort of horses were selling for 80 to 100 guineas and even carriage horses were being sold for just under that amount.

TRAINERS

TOM STEBBING GREEN

In 1875 Tom Stebbing Green arrived in Beverley to set up as a trainer and registered his colours of a black jacket with red sleeves and cap.

He used the gallops on the Westwood most of the time but took his string to Hambleton during the summer months when the gallops became rock hard.

Tom was a very busy person, as he was a member of the Beverley Town Council for many years, on one occasion he had to give evidence on behalf of the Beverley Corporation in the House of Commons. He was also above average cricketer and played for Hull and later Scarborough. He had an average of 40 runs per innings; he also represented Scarborough, against an all-England team.

Whilst Tom was good with horses, he had no head for business. He never kept books, and often made notes of expenditure on race-cards or bits of paper. An example of his easy-going manner in relation to finance was when he visited his local butcher on his way home from the races. He ordered three or four stones of beef, when asked if he would like a bill, Tom replied, "I want Na bills, when the last £20 I gave you is done, let me know and I'll give you another to be going on with".

In 1876 a year after his arrival at Beverley he trained a three year old chestnut colt by *Blair Atholl* for the second Earl of Durham, and won six races out of seven with him. The following year he won the Watt Memorial at Beverley for the Earl.

He was also an expert billiards player and was a well known player in the clubs of Hull. On one occasion there was a foreign gentleman awaiting his ship, so spent the time playing billiards in one of the clubs near the dock. He was playing and beating all the good local players, so the manager of the club wired Tom and asked him to come down as soon as possible, and save the situation.

Tom strolled in, picked up a cue and made a few shots; he was soon given a challenge by the foreign gentleman. The stakes were quite small at first, and Tom was well beaten. Later when they got to £300, Tom's opponent proposed a double or quits game. This was exactly what Tom and the rest of the club members were waiting for, Tom won the match easily and collected the money and made his way back to Beverley.

He also kept greyhounds whilst living in Beverley, and had some very good ones.

Tom left Beverley, to take up residency at the Hambleton Hotel; he was mine host and yet still found time to train racehorses. He died in 1899 at the age of 83 years of age. Tom was buried in the church yard at Cold Kirby.

After Green's death, his nephew, William Thornton, who rode a good deal for Tom, and was a strong and determined horseman, took over the reigns. He remained at Hambleton for a while with just a few horses, but later went to Hednesford and then to Beverley. He never had much success as a trainer, and later acted as stud-groom to Sir Lycett Green and died in Beverley in 1948.

In the mid 1800's one of the many legendary characters to have been closely associated with racing at Beverley was a certain Robert Ridsdale. He was formerly a groom in Yorkshire but soon became a professional gambler and was without doubt one of the most flamboyant swindler's in the history of the turf. He lived near to the course, and rarely missed a meeting at the Westwood. And despite his humble origins, he played the role of a cultivated gentleman with great aplomb.

In 1832 he owned the 1832 Derby winner, *St Giles* in partnership with John Gully who was a working class Gloucestershire born champion boxer. The partnership was marked by controversy, and many suspected the pair of unfairly influencing races. However the Derby prize of £47.0000 further fuelled Ridsdale's extravagant lifestyle. Unfortunately, Robert was eventually found dead in a Newmarket stable with just three halfpence in his pocket.

WILLIAM 'BILL' SCOTT

The mention of *St Giles* Derby victory, brings us to the colts rider, William Scott, known to everyone as 'Bill', who was the brother of the renowned Malton trainer, John Scott.

'Bill' had his first public ride in 1814 when he rode at 6stone 10lbs on *Belville* and his final ride was at York on Mr Conway's *Snowball* in 1847, the year before his death.

It was in 1846 that he was involved in controversy in that years running of the Derby, the horse involved was named *Sir Tatton Sykes* and was owned by 'Bill'. The colt was bred near Driffield by a farmer named Hudson, the colt ran as a two year old under the name of *Tibthorpe*. But was later re-named by Scott, after Sir Tatton Sykes, the 4th Baronet and notable breeder of thoroughbreds at Sledmere. 'Bill' had an argument with his brother John who was training the colt, as a result he sent the colt to be trained by William Oates, although he probable trained the colt himself. In the Derby, *Sir Tatton Sykes* was ridden by 'Bill' and as he took the colt to the start, it was clear to everyone that he had consumed far too much alcohol and at the start he argued with the starter, however after more than one false start, the field set off. It was quite clear to most that he was unable to even steer the horse on a proper course, and was beaten in a race he really should have won. That year, he did however win the oldest classic race, the St Leger. This was to be his final victory in the race, he still holds the record for most winning rides in the race, which totalled nine and during his career he rode a total of nineteen Classic winners.

He died just over two years later on the 26th October 1848 at Highfield House, Malton and his remains were thought to be in the Church yard at Meaux near to Beverley, but they were in fact, buried in a vault under the aisle of Wawne Church not far from Beverley.

JOHN SCOTT 1794 - 1871

During his career, John Scott trained for many notable owners, including the 14th Earl of Derby, the 6th Viscount Falmouth and John Bowes, Bowes was a member of the Jockey Club and a very wealthy man, who loved horse racing.

He also trained for Edward Petre of Stapleton Park in Darrington parish, North Yorkshire, Petre also owned Whitewall Stables in Malton. When Petre went bankrupt in the early 1840's, Scott acquired the premises.

Between 1827 and 1863, John Scott won a record forty British Classic Races, and in 1853 he became the first trainer to win the English Triple Crown when his colt *West Australian* won the 2.000 guineas, the Epsom Derby, and the St Leger Stakes.

John Scott died on the 4th October 1871 and his funeral was attended by racing folk from far and wide. It appeared that the entire population of Malton and Norton either took part in the procession or lined the streets to witness the event. The procession left Whitewall House at eleven o'clock and included a great number of gentlemen from the town and surrounding area walking four abreast. They were followed by mounted Police Superintendents from Driffield, Malton and Norton. Apparently the body was enclosed in three coffins, the outer one being made of polished oak. Attached was a breast plate with the following simple inscription, "John Scott, born November 30th 1794; died October 4th 1871". A subscription fund was started in London for a public monument, which was finally erected three years later in Malton Cemetery and was made from granite and Sicilian marble and stands twenty feet high.

On the death of John Scott, John Bowes one of his previously mentioned wealthy owners and who lived at Streatlam Castle, had taken the lease on Langton Wold, it was here that his horses continued to be trained. He loved horse racing, but was a curious character, he had owned four Derby winners, but rarely went to the races. On one of the rare occasions he did so George Fordham who rode for him, didn't even know him by sight. When he did make an appearance on the racecourse, he asked George Fordham how one of his animals had run, and was rebuked by the jockey who thought he was a punter touting for information.

The training operations at Langton Wold however were very much at risk, Mr Bowes leased the property from the Reverend Norcliffe, who was faced with conscientious scruples as to whether he could receive, let alone enjoy, the income derived from the training of racehorses. Fortunately for all concerned, wiser counsels prevailed and the Reverend was persuaded that he was doing nothing "illegal", or contrary to ecclesiastical law, morals or order, by sanctioning the training of racehorses on his property. No doubt the Reverend Norcliffe was advised by at least two of fellow East Yorkshire clerics who at that time had horses in training. It was also apparent that some of the top land owners, keen followers of the hunt had had some say in the matter, so the threat to this great training area was put aside.

MARSON FAMILY

Job Marson senior, the trainer of *Nancy* was also a former jockey and his son certainly followed in his fathers foot-steps. Job junior was born at Norton the East Riding side of Malton. He was a brilliant jockey who rode the winner of the Derby and the St Leger on more than one occasion. When he won the 1851 Derby on *Teddington* for Sir Joseph Hawley, he did so in a canter, even though the colt had his problems in his preparation for Epsom.

One of Job's Derby winners was when he rode for Lord Zetland,who owned the mighty *Voltigeur*, he was bred by Robert Stephenson at his stud at Hart, near Hartlepool, County Durham. As a yearling he was sent to the sales, but failed to attract a bid and was returned to Mr Stephenson. Robert Hill the private trainer to Lord Zetland was impressed by the colt and eventually persuaded Lord Zetland to buy him the following autumn for £1.000. The sale arrangement provided for an extra £500 to be paid if the colt won the Derby. Hill took charge of training the colt at Aske, North Yorkshire.

As a two year old he only ran once, winning the Wright Stakes at Richmond, North Yorkshire on the 31st of October 1849. He looked impressive in the paddock and won well. As a three year old, *Voltigeur* went straight for the Derby, however prior to the race Lord Zetland discovered that the colt's breeder had not made the correct entry payments and that it would cost a further £400 to run in the Derby. His Lordship was determined to withdraw the horse, however, when it was explained that many of his Yorkshire tenants had wagered heavily on the horse and faced ruin if he failed to win or worse still, not even run, he relented. Job settled the colt in seventh place, before making his challenge in the home straight and ran on strongly to win by a length over the favourite *Clincher.* His odds of 16-1 were very rewarding for all Lord Zetland's tenants.

The following September, *Voltigeur* returned to Yorkshire for the St Leger at Doncaster. He started favourite at odds of 8-13, from the off the other riders attempted to 'box' him in against the rails. Job decided to change tactics, and attempted to win from the front. In the late stages of the race, the colt tired and was caught in the closing stages of the race. The judge declared a dead heat, and with the owners of the two colts failing to reach an agreement to divide the stakes, the colts had to race again over the same course later that afternoon. Trainer Hill planned to rest *Voltigeur* in his stable before the re-match, but was advised by the great trainer of Classics, John Scott that if he did so he "might as well shoot him through the head" as he would stiffen up. Hill therefore took Scott's advice and kept *Voltigeur* walking round, until called for the race. In the second race Job was able to employ waiting tactics, and tracked *Russborough* before moving ahead inside the final furlong to win comfortably by a length. Not content to having *Voltigeur* running almost four miles in one day, connections entered him for the Scarborough Stakes the following day, where fortunately he won by 'walking over'. And despite his exertions, he turned out two days later for the Doncaster Cup, for which only the 1849 winner of the Derby and St Leger, *The Flying Dutchman* who was un-beaten in thirteen career starts was the only opponent. *The Flying Dutchman's* jockey appeared to be the worse for drink and Marson was able bide his time on *Voltigeur*, before pulling ahead to win by half a length to cause a huge upset.

Job settled in Spennithorne near Middlham where he and his wife lived in a little property that he had bought after being given £2.000 present for winning the Derby in 1851 on *Teddington* for Sir Joseph Hawley. He was quite a young man when he died and he and his wife are buried in the village graveyard

His son Job the third, had a brief and somewhat inglorious career, dying at Thirsk on December 11th 1870 at the age of twenty five.

PAT TAYLOR

Pat Taylor took out a licence to train in 1949. He rented a small yard in York Road, Beverley, which was owned by the Beverley Racecourse Committee, These premises were next to Captain Storey's York Road stables, before moving to much larger premises at Northlands, Walkington, about two miles from the York Road Stables. Pat sent out over 500 winners during his 36 year training career. One of his particular favourites, and that of the local punters was a horse named *Penitent*, who won twenty races in all, and finished his career at his local track when he won the Tote Investers Handicap, and in doing so beat the track record at the ripe old age of 13 years. Another stalwart of the yard was a filly named *Soraya* she won quite a number of races, Pat Taylor used a little used method to calm her down at home and Pat attributed her improved form due to introducing a goat to her box. It made her much settled and contented and the goat even accompanied the filly to the races, including to Beverley, which was barely a mile or so from her stable. As an aside, one of Pat's stable hands was a Beverley born young lady called Jo, who was later to marry Jack Berry. Pat left Walkington in 1966 and set up a stable in Goldalming, Surrey. However he was soon on the move again, finally settling up at Lambourn, where he had many successes, including, *Tip the Wink* who won the Arkle Chase at Cheltenham in 1977. Pat finally retired in 1985.

JAMES "Jimmy" THOMPSON

Jimmy was born in the North East in 1917 and became one of the leading Jockey's in the North. He did not inherit any of his formidable skill from his family, as none of them had any remote connection with horse racing. However, from a very young age, Jimmy was determined to succeed in his chosen profession. This fact was vividly illustrated, when at the age of thirteen and standing just four feet six inches tall, he set off to France to take up an apprenticeship with the French Trainer Juan Tortorolo, who had advertised the vacancy in one of England's sporting papers. So Jimmy barely a teenager set off on his own to Chantilly, in France. Tortorolo soon recognised the ability of this very young but determined English boy, and gave him an early opportunity to ride in public. His faith was not wasted and Jimmy was the leading apprentice, riding more than 100 winners. Unfortunately,

R. Boynton riding Penitent to victory at Beverley in July 1959
for trainer Pat Taylor

Jimmy had to cut short his time in France, to return home due to the outbreak of World War Two.

After the war he worked for Gerald Armstrong at Middleham, later moving to trainers R. Robson and Ernie Davey. He was able to go to the scales at 7stone 9 pounds and had no need to waste, and was very much in demand. In 1950 at the age of thirty three, he was crowned the leading rider of the Scottish circuit and rode over twenty five winners beating Bill Nevett by just over eight victories.

In 1954 he was riding at Newcastle when the horse in front of his mount kicked up a stone which hit Jimmy in the eye, blinding him in one eye. This incident affectively ended his riding career.

Jimmy eventually took up training, and was based at various parts of the Country, Beverley, Shiptonthorpe Newby Hall, Ripon, and Newmarket. At Beverley in 1956 until 1962 he trained from Pasture Terrace, and his daughter Jane would ride out for him, eventually she would take up employment at 'Snowy' Gray's York Road stables. She was a very competent rider and did ride in races confined to Amateurs. In the meantime Jimmy was to taste success at his local course of Beverley, when the filly *Virgin Queen* won for her local owner Bob Headley, she won comfortable despite dislodging her jockey before the start. Jimmy's future Son-in Law was in the Stands that day and witnessed the sparkling display put in by the filly. So it was with a great deal of confidence that Paul and a few of his mates, set foot in a betting shop at Bridlington to invest a few 'bob' on *Virgin Queen* a few days after her run at Beverley. By good fortune I.T.V were showing horse racing that day and the *Virgin Queen's* race was being featured. Television screens had not yet reached the betting shops, so the lads found a Television/Radio sales shop, nearby so they stood outside, glued to the shop window. Coming to the last furlong *Virgin Queen* took up the running and the noise from the viewers outside the shop, must have been heard in Scarborough. The owner of the shop must have been disturbed by this football type crowd and decided to end the viewing and the cheering, and promptly pulled the plug on the race, with all the sets on display going blank. The lads then set off probably faster than *Virgin Queen* to the betting shop, just in time to hear the filly had won the race

It was his spell at Newby Hall, near Ripon a stable he had taken over from Billy Nevett that he trained the popular *Copper Horse* whom he successfully placed to win on no less than 12 occasions, a phenomenal record.

In the 1965/1966 season Jimmy was appointed as the private trainer to David Robinson a British entrepreneur and philanthropist who made his vast fortune by renting out radio's and television's and who had spent lots of money on both bloodstock and stables in Newmarket. Jimmy was based at the Carlburgh stables, in the 1967 season, which ironically proved to be his last for David Robinson. He trained well over thirty winners that season and his thirtieth winner being the talented two year old *So Blessed.* who went on to win the July Cup and Nunthorpe Stakes when trained the following season by Michael Jarvis. Another of Jimmy's winners was *Enrico* who won the prestigeous Victoria Cup in 1966.

Jimmy returned to being a public trainer at stables in Wetherby and finally at Colerne, near, Chippenham, Wiltshire, where he trained that brilliant sprinter *Raffingora,* before Bill Marshall took over both the horse and the stable.

GEOFF TOFT

Geoff was a trainer in the late 1960's early 70's and trained at the stable known as the Kings Arms Stable, a former coaching house which Geoff purchased in 1968 for the princely sum of £1.500. The stable was situated behind the Royal Standard Public House, North Bar Within Beverley. The Head Lad for Geoff at that time was George Margarson now a leading Newmarket racehorse trainer and another leading Newmarket trainer who looked after *Gunner B* most of the time when trained by Geoff, was Paul D'Arcy. Steve Lawes was Geoff's apprentice and rode several winners, one of Steve's favourites was the colt *Superior Class* trained by Geoff. In September 1977 carrying the feather weight of seven stone seven pound in a Nursery Handicap he provided Steve with his first ever win at Chester a tricky course to ride even for an experienced rider. *Superior Class* had provided Steve with two wins from four rides, having won a seller at Thirsk in the July of 1977. This Beverley based rider had a very lucky escape from serious injury in May 1979 when riding *Tallishire Tommy*, when his mount clipped the heels of the horse he was following, he was thrown and 'buried' by the rest of the field after spending four days in Doncaster Royal Infirmary he was allowed home after suffering facial cuts, concussion and a hairline fracture of the vertebrae. Steve is now a work rider for Tim Easterby. Steve's son, Nicky, started life as an apprentice jockey and rode his first winner at Beverley for Richard Fahey the Malton trainer.

Previously Geoff was travelling head lad for that very successful trainer, the Malton based Pat Rohan before moving to Beverley. Geoff's stable produced a number of winners, particularly for local owners. He persuaded Paul Downey to purchase a filly from him, which was named *Bouchette.* This was Paul's first venture into horse racing and the filly won many races for him, one of these successes was at his local track on the Westwood and Paul recalls that he spent most of the winnings on champagne. The filly certainly paid her way as she also won races over hurdles.

However the best horse Geoff trained was the

home bred entire *Gunner B,* he broke the horse in and won some very good handicaps with him. However in 1978 the owner moved the colt to Newmarket to be trained by Henry Cecil and in his first 4 races, he won four Group races, which included the Group 1 Eclipse Stakes.

Gunner B was a homebred and was bred by Mr J Barrett and raced in the colours of his wife Mrs P Barrett. He was trained at Beverley, behind the Royal Standard Public House in North Bar Within, by Geoff Toft, the colt was broken by Paul D'Arcy who looked after him throughout *Gunner B's* time with Geoff.

At two years of age, he raced seven times winning at Newcastle and Doncaster. At three the colt ran ten times and was placed in nine of the races, winning five of them, which included the Watt Memorial Handicap Stakes at Beverley, the Cecil Frail Handicap at Haydock Park and the Doonside Cup at Ayr. It may be of interest to the reader that he was being ridden by Joe Mercer, who was later to become first jockey to Henry Cecil.

So in 1978 the owner decided to send him to Henry Cecil. *Gunner B* made further progress under his trainer Henry Cecil and won four Group races, including the valuable Eclipse Stakes. He finished second in the Benson and Hedges at York, and won at Goodwood before ending his racing career by coming second in the prestigious Champion Stakes at Newmarket. Commenting on *Gunner B's* apparent improvement, Henry Cecil thought the reason for it, was that he could work the entire with higher class horses.

He also thought that the reason he beat better

horses than himself, was because he was so genuine.

He retired to stud in 1979 and throughout his stud career was responsible for a large number of winners on the flat and over the jumps. Including producing over 100 winners whilst covering mares in West Germany.

At the age of 31 years, he was about to enter his 25th year at stud, when he passed away. *Gunner B* was without doubt one of the best racehorses to come out of a Beverley yard.

KARL BURKE

Is based at the famous establishment known as Spigot Lodge so named after the 1921 winner of the St Leger *Jack Spigot*. In the not too distant past, Sam Hall, Colonel Lyde and Chris Thornton sent out so many big race winners and they are being followed by an equally astute trainer Karl Burke able assisted by his wife Elaine. Karl and his wife are committed to an on-going development of Spigot Lodge and are well aware of it's racing history. Karl was particularly pleased to train *Libertarian* to win the Dante at York in 2013, as it was the first winner of the Dante to be trained in Yorkshire for 70 years.

MICK EASTERBY

Mick, the younger brother of Peter was born on the 30th March 1931, he also combined farming with training horses and in 1961 started with about a dozen horses, he also trained under both codes and gained his first winner when *Great Rock* owned by Mrs A.C Straker and ridden by Jimmy Etherington won a mile and half handicap at Edinburgh. In 1977 Mick gained his only Classic winner when *Mrs McArdy* won the 1.000 guineas. Mick was asked to look for a horse by one of his owners a Mr Kettlewell and sold him Mrs McArdy for a £1000 and at the December sales in 1977 she was sold for £154.000 to Bert Firestone, and was booked to go to a top stallion in America. He had other notable winners on the flat with *Lochnager*, winner of the King Stand Stakes, July Cup, Nunthorpe and Temple Stakes, all Group races which showed how Mick could train class horses. In 1976 he showed his versatality by training *Peterhof* to win the hugely competative Triumph Hurdle at Cheltenham ridden by Jonjo O'Neil.

Many stories have been told regarding the Easterby Brother, some are even true. However I like the one involving Lester Piggott. He had just ridden him a winner and asked the trainer, "Where's my present". The trainer replied, "But I'm only a poor farmer, I can't afford to give you a present". Lester quickly came back with the reply, "Give me a sack of potatoes then".

One of Mick's first owners was a Holderness farmer, the late Charlie Buckton, Charlie was also the breeder of race horses at his farm at Rise.

CAPTAIN CHARLES FREDERICK ELSEY

The Captain was born in Lincolnshire in 1882, his brother became a bishop, but Charles assisted his father, William Edward Elsey at Baumber, Lincolnshire before he commenced training in his own right in 1911 at Middleham. He then saw service in the First World War with the Yorkshire Hussars and the Royal Berks. Upon leaving the Forces he took up training at Ayr in Scotland before taking up training at his beloved Highfield near Malton. He trained his first ever winner at Beverley and a race was later named in his honour.

Captain Elsey was the leading trainer in the north and was Champion trainer on eight occasions. He won six classic races, the first in 1949 when *Musidora* won the 1000 guineas and followed up by winning the Oaks. He then trained the Oaks winner with *Frieze* in 1952 and the following year he trained *Nearula* to win the 2.000 guineas. In 1956 he won the 1.000 guineas again with *Honeylight* and his final classic winner came with *Cantelo* who won the St Leger.

Musidora the Captain's dual classic winner in 1949 was sent to the 1947 Doncaster Sales, where she was bought for 4.700 guineas by a Scottish shipping magnate Norman Donaldson. He sent the filly to Captain Elsey to be trained at his Highfield Stables at Malton and she became his first ever classic winner. *Musidora* began her three year-old season at the now defunct course at Stockton-on Tees, when she won the Roseberry Stakes. She was then sent to Newmarket for the 1000 guineas and ridden by Edgar Britt, she won by one an half lengths from the favourite *Unknown Quantity.* The following month when 4-1 favourite she won in a time two seconds faster than that recorded by *Nimbus* in winning the Derby over the same course and distance two days later.

Captain Elsey, loved racing his horses at Beverley and trained for some local owners. One of the old time favourites was the grey, *Crusador's Horn* who was owned by a local chemist Mr A. L. Spinks. Captain Elsey described as "The gamest horse I ever trained". He was purchased for only 420 guineas as a yearling in 1944 and became a real favourite of the punters, especially at Beverley where he won seven races and even won on consecutive days at the June meeting of 1948, he was ridden on both occasions by the Australian jockey Edgar Britt. Later that year he won yet another race on the Westwood, incidentally the following day the Captain had three winners, in the crowd to witness the achievement that day was none other than the Duke of Norfolk one of the Chief Stewards of the Jockey Club.

When he finally retired in the early 1960's his son, an ex-fighter pilot took over the reigns. Bill made a great success of the job.

JIMMY FITZGERALD

Jimmy was born appropriately in a village in County Tipperary, Ireland call Horse and Jockey in 1935.

He was a real horseman and before taking up training was a very good jump jockey. He won the Scottish Grand National in 1965 on *Brasher*, unfortunately the following year he sustained a skull fracture which ended his career.

He joined the training ranks in 1969 and enjoyed great success from his Malton yard both on the flat and over the sticks. He trained six Festival winners including the 1985 Gold Cup with *Forgive* 'n Forget, which also won the Irish Hennessy in 1987, with stable jockey and Yorkshire based Mark Dwyer on board, a race that incidentally Mark won a further three times when riding *Jodami* for the Yorkshire farmer/trainer Peter Beaumont in 1993,1994 and 1995. He also won the English Hennessy in 1985 when Mark rode *Galway Blaze* for Jimmy. Jimmy also won the Scottish Grand National as a trainer in 1984 and again in 1985 with the same horse *Androma.*

On the flat, he trained well over 300 winners, which included the Princess of Wales Group 2 race at Newmarket with *Sapience* in the 1990 season; the same horse won the Ebor Handicap in the previous season, on both occasions with the late Pat Eddery on board. Jimmy also sent out the winner of the Cesarewitch on two occasions with *Kayudee* in 1985 and *Trainglot* in 1990, earlier that season he had taken the Lincoln Handicap with *Evichstar* at odds of 33-1 with the very useful Yorkshire based lightweight Alan Munro doing the riding honours, Alan went on to become an International Jockey of the highest order.

W.H.GRAY

William Harrison Gray better known to most as 'Snowy', started his career in racing as an apprentice jockey with Sir John Renwick at Malton. He later was to ride several winners as a National Hunt jockey. After his riding career had ended, he joined Captain James Storrie at the York Road stables, in Beverley, and was the Captain's Head Lad for over twenty five years. When the Captain was appointed Clerk of the Course at Beverley, he took over the licence from the Captain in the early 1950's and with his son Clifford as his head lad. He enjoyed plenty of success over the years, including many winners for Scottish owners. He trained *Lucky* Brief to win the Dante at York in 1962 and again in 1965 with *Ballymarais* when ridden by the Australian born jockey Bill Pyers. In the 1965 Epsom Derby he ran two colts, *Ballymarais* again ridden by Bill Pyers who finished 7th at 25-1 and *Sunacelli* ridden by stable jockey Brian Connorton who finished 17th of the 22 runners, the race was won by the great *Sea--Bird* a French horse, who was trained by Ettienne Pollet. *Sea-Bird* was later to win the Prix de l'Arc de Triumphe in a facile manner. 'Snowy' was a man of very few words and one of his favourite sayings was, "When you win, say little"; "When you lose, say nothing".

Lucky Brief winning the Watt Memorial at Beverley for local trainer Snowy Gray and Jockey Brian Connorton in June 1963.

'Snowy's' blacksmith at that time, was a Beverley man, John Chapleo, on one particular day he arrived at the stable and was approached by a young man and a lady. They were in a small van and he asked John if would be all right to park outside the stable in York Road.

John asked the reason for the visit, and the young man told him they had come to Beverley to visit his former neighbour from Liverpool, Eric Apter, a jockey with Mr Gray. John, having established they were bone fide visitors, found a place for them to park the van, and informed the young man that Eric was on the gallops but would be returning shortly. As it was a bitterly cold morning he suggested they should wait in the saddle room and to stoke up the fire.

John was in the yard when Eric returned with several others and told him of the visitors. Eric, went off to see them in the saddle room, he later made a point of thanking John for looking after the couple, John asked him who they were, Eric replied quite casually, they were Paul McCartney and Linda who was either his wife, or wife to be, (they were married in London in 1969) As this event took place in the late 1960's it was at a time when the Beatles were household names, and John couldn't believe that Paul was driving a 'tatty' van on his visit to Beverley. Paul must have been an ardent supporter of the 'Sport of Kings' as in the 1960's he bought his father a horse called *Drake's Drum* and was pleased to lead it into the winners enclosure at his local track at Aintree.

BILLY HAMMETT

Billy Hammett was born at Exeter and began riding for Pat Hartingan and another trainer called Mr O. Anthony before making the journey north to ride for Captain S.C Henderson at Hexham. Billy was for many seasons a leading National Hunt jockeys and on one memorable occasion rode a particular bad jumper at Carlisle, the inevitable happened and his mount fell, however Billy remounted and despite having a cut lip and being badly shaken, he went on to win the race. The owner's present for Billy's exploits, was a packet of cigarettes.

When Billy retired from the saddle he set up as a trainer at Ripon, before taking a similar role at Sir Lycett Green's near York. He moved to Beverley

Billy Hammett outside his Beverely Home

in 1925 at stables situated in Pasture Terrace, very near to the Westwood. He never had many horses to train and none would be top class. But he did have a top class owner, in the shape of Stanley Mathews, who in 1965 was knighted for his services to football. Stanley had a horse in training with Billy, in the early 1950's named *Parbleu* and Stanley often travelled to Beverley to watch his horse work on the tan gallops of the Westwood. Billy handed in his trainers licence in, at the end of the 1955 season, however he was not lost to horse racing as he took up the position of Assistant Trainer to Peter Ward who at the age of 22 years was at that time one of the youngest trainers in the Country, he leased Billy's stable after searching for a bigger place than he had at Doncaster. In January 1956 tragedy struck when Peter and his wife Jill were on their way to Leicester races, they were negotiating a bend when a head on collision occurred. Peter who was only 24 years old at the time died in the accident and wife Jill suffered concussion and cuts to the head. One of the first people on the scene was fellow trainer Tommy Dent a trainer who was also on his way to Leicester.

Billy Hammett had a side line that proved very popular and sought after by his fellow trainers, he sold a mixture that apparently cured horses of the cough. He refused to divulge the recipe to any other person and he took the recipe to his grave.

However, I digress, back to Peter who was the son of trainer Bob Ward who trained at Hednesford, near Stafford and quite clearly Peter had a promising career in front of him, His wife Jill, later re-married and she established the highly successful Aike Grange Stud at Aike a small hamlet between Beverley and Driffield.

MARK JOHNSTON

A former veterinary surgeon began his training career in 1987 with a handful of horses in Lincolnshire. He moved to the famous Kingsley House stables in Middleham, Yorkshire in 1988. his first winner was *Hinari Video*, one of five winners he managed that year. His theory from the outset to be successful was quite simple, "there's nothing that makes you train winners, like an overdraft". This was followed by the motto of the stable, "Always trying". These ideals served him well in the years ahead and from these very humble beginnings he never looked back. He would go on to train a record century of winners each season, and on four occasions trained a double century of winners in a season. Classic, Ascot, Goodwood together with winners abroad came thick and fast, and his skill was soon recognised by the Al Maktoum Royal Family of Dubai, who sent him horses to train.

What is highly significant and really highlights the progress of this Scottish born trainer is the prize money he has earned for his owners, his five winners in 1988 brought in a total of £10.895 in winning prize money. However since then, the majority of seasons, the stable has earned it's owners in excess of £1 million in prize money.

PAUL MIDGELEY

Paul was always going to be involved in horse racing, he could ride from an early age and loved show jumping and hunting. At sixteen years of age he travelled the short distance from his home to join trainer Paul Blockley and he soon rode his first National Hunt winner and over the next three or four years he had accumulated over thirty winners. Having to continually shed excess weight made his racing life uncomfortable, so he retired from race riding and started a livery and breaking yard. In 2003 he took out a licence to train on the family farm near Malton and soon started sending out the winners. Over the past five seasons he has trained over 300 winners, he is constantly trying to improve the quality as well as the quantity of racehorse he trains, more will be heard of this hardworking trainer.

JAMIE OSBORNE

Was born in Cottingham near Hull and was reputedly to be Her Majesty the Queen Mother's favourite National Hunt jockey. Jamie is now a successful trainer, he took out his first licence to train in the year 2000. It only took him three years for him to train his first Group 1 winner when *Milk it Mick* won the Dewhurst Stakes at Newmarket for the millionaire owner Paul Dixon, Darryl Holland was the jockey on board.

However, on the 29th March 2014, at the Maydan racecourse in Dubai the combination of two Jamie's, Osborne the trainer and Spencer the jockey, came up to win one of the world's big races, the United Arab Emerites Derby with *Toast of New York* a feature of the race was out of the first eight home seven were ridden by U.K based jockeys and five of those eight were trained by U.K based trainers. Jamie Osborne had certainly arrived as a trainer to watch for the future. Incidentally *Toast of New York* was owned by a man mainly associated with the jumping game, Michael Buckley. However the prize money of £722,891,57 for winning the U.A.E Derby was likely to encourage Michael to enjoy the flat racing scene much more.

PAT ROHAN

Pat came to this Country in 1957 from his native Ireland to ride in a selling hurdle race at the request of trainer Freddie Maxwell. The horse was owned by the great actor of his time Robert Morley and though the horse ran unplaced Pat found a place to stay as Freddie's Assistant at a time that Freddie was producing lots of big race winners. Mention of Robert Morley, I must inform you of a clause that he had written into his contracts, wherever he was performing he would not be available to do matinee's on Derby Day, unfortunately and ironically he passed away aged 84 years in 1992 on Derby Day.

However, I digress yet again, back to Pat Rohan, his next move was due to a chance meeting he had on Warwick railway station with Rupert Watson (who in 1968 became Lord Manton on the death of his father) Rupert was on his way to London to visit his Doctor and Pat was on his way back home to Ireland, Rupert suddenly remembered he had left his wallet with his valet in the weighing room at Warwick racecourse. Pat checked his wallet

Photo shows Pat Rowan recieving the Owbridge Sprint Trophy on behalf of Irish bloodstock agent, Bertie Kerr after his Desert Call had won The Big Sprint Race at Beverley in August 1968

and found he had £20 which he shared with Rupert which was enough to see them both to there chosen destination. Rupert then asked what he was busy with and would he be interested in working for him and his wife, and as he put it, to baby sit and look after his hunters. He also invited Pat to bring his hunter back from Ireland and he could then hunt with The Belvoir. Pat was soon back in England and his friendship with the future Lord and Lady Manton would stand the test of time. Pat's next move was again as a result of a chance meeting, this time with Tim Molony the great National Hunt jockey. Tim told Pat that Bill Dutton was looking for an Assistant Trainer and if he was interested he would arrange for a meeting between the two. They met at Southwell races and after a brief meeting Pat was offered the job.

Pat arrived in Malton and soon got cracking in

his new role, he also rode out for other trainers, one being the ex-jockey Dick Curran. Pat was to ride his first ever Chase winner, when he rode Dick's, Polished Steel in a 3 mile event at the now defunct course at Manchester. Bill and Pat had a great summer together, however it all ended on a sad note when Bill passed away suddenly in the December1958. So, on the 1st January 1959 Pat took over the licence of Grove Cottage Stable. Bill was renowned for training big race winners, and it wasn't long before Pat followed in his footsteps. A year later Pat married Bill Dutton's daughter, Mary, and between them they sent out a number of big race winners. Among them was two speedsters *Right Boy* which Bill Dutton had purchased as a yearlong for the sum of 575 guineas the other one of the fastest sprinters ever, *Pappa Fourway,* who cost less than *Right Boy,* these sprinters won races both in the north and south, Pat was particular pleased to come back from his forays in the south with a big race win under his belt. He trained *Right Boy* to win the July Cup, the King George Stakes the Cork and Ornery Stakes, the King Stand Stakes as well as two Nunthorpe's

Pat Rohan and his wife Mary at their home in Malton in 2015

at York. But Pat could also handle stayers as well, in his first year of training he won the Brown Jack Stakes at Ascot with *Sandiacre* ridden by Lester Piggott.

He ended his training career in Bahrain after being appointed private trainer to the Emir of Bahrain.

Finally, I should mention that Bill Dutton apart from being a first class trainer, he also achieved a high level of success as a jockey, particularly in 1928 when he rode the winner of The Grand National riding the £50 bargain horse, *Tipperary Tim* at 100-1, the only other horse to finish that year after being re-mounted was *Billy Barton*.

ALFRED SMITH

Everyone knew Mr Smith, as Alf. He was a Yorkshireman through and through and a plain speaking individual. He was brought up on a farm with working horses and apart from a short break, when he was appointed Head Groundsman at Beverley Racecourse, trained them for many years. He took out a licence in 1951 to train, and throughout his career never trained more than a dozen or so horses. His first stable in Beverley was Pasture House, in Pasture Terrace overlooking the Westwood, he later moved to Heath House stables again adjacent to the Westwood on the Newbald Road. He, had a very keen eye for a bargain buy and most of his horses were cheaply bought. An example of the sort Alf purchased were, *Flying Diplomat* at 1000 guineas, who won six races on the flat and surprised many people when winning the Imperial Cup at Sandown

Park and was only beaten a neck in the Scheppes. *Flying Tyke* cost only 500 guineas and won 5 sprint races on the 'bounce' as a three year old. *Vewilin* another 500 guineas purchase won eleven jump races and *Turi* a bargain buy at 250 guineas won races on the flat and over jumps.

In 1977 Alf achieved a life's time ambition when he saddled *Top Straight* to win the Newmarket Town Plate, when ridden to perfection by his then, Assistant Trainer, Hilary Jack. So Alf having ridden *Tip It In* as a young boy, for local cattle dealer, Harry Dawson to win the Kiplingcotes Derby had achieved success in two of the oldest races in England.

However the yard hit the headlines in 1993 when they turned out *Cape Merino* to win the

Beverley trainers meet at Beverley Racecourse - Left to right John Booth, Alf Smith, Snowy Gray, Pat Taylor and Sid Renton Racecourse Managing Director

Redcar Sprint Trophy for two year olds at 33-1. She was a filly bought cheaply by Alf and the stable received about £190.000 in prize money and bonuses. It was whilst Alf was ill in hospital that the owner Mrs Dianne Ellis removed *Cape Marino* and two other horses from the stable and sent them to be trained at West Ilsley by David Chappell. Alf's wife Elma described the situation as "very disapointing".

Alf passed away in 2001 in hospital and Paul Wood a local farmer who had been assisting Alf, was granted a temporary licence to train.

CAPTAIN JC STORRIE

Captain Storrie trained in Beverley for many years, mainly for Mr Wilson of the Ellerman Wilson shipping line. He gave training up, to work at the Beverley racecourse, he became Chairman in the late 1940's and was in charge on that record breaking day in 1946 when nearly 28.000 spectators crammed onto the course. He was later joined by Sidney Renton who, for 30 years as Secretary and Director took the benefits of Beverley to a wider audience. It was Mr Renton who persuaded the Hull bookmaker George Habbershaw (who when only 14 years of age, ran all the way from Beverley railway station, to the racecourse to have his first bet) to sponsor a race, he was to be followed by the Needler family, Robert B Massey and the Jackson Group of companies, some of whom are still sponsoring races to this day.

Captain Storrie in a Pensive Mood

SAM HALL

Sam was the youngest of three brothers who all went on to be extremely good trainers of horses. He was a typical out-spoken Yorkshire man, and when based at his Brecongill Stables, Middleham, sent out the winners at most of the major racecourses, including Royal Ascot, the Dewhurst Stakes and a couple of Cesarewitch winners at Newmarket, two Ebor winners at York, the Ayr Gold Cup the November Handicap on five occasions, the Zetland Cup on four occasions, together with three Andy Capp Handicaps at

Redcar. Plus other big races, Sam loved to win the big handicap races and in all trained over a thousand winners.

Sam started out assisting his two brothers, before taking out his licence in 1949, and started training at Brecongill Stables before moving to Spigot Lodge at Leyburn, North Yorkshire, in 1967. His two daughters were heavily involved in horse racing, Kate Walton trains under both codes at Sharp Hill Farm, Middleham, and Liz was Secretary to Guy Reed at both his Studs at Nidd Hall and Copgrove Hall. His niece Sally occupies the historic Brecongill Stables.

Charlie Hall, the middle one of the three brothers was also a brilliant trainer, particularly over the jumps and is annually remembered at Wetherby every October when the valuable and prestigious Charlie Hall Chase takes place. His stable at Towton near Wetherby was taken over by his stepson Maurice Camacho, before moving to the Star Cottage Stable at Malton in 1981. The stable is now in the hands of Maurice's daughter Julie and she is assisted by her husband Steve whom she married in 1998.

JACK BERRY MBE

Jack Berry was born on October 7th 1937 in Leeds he was the fourth member of a family of eight, and as a youngster he described himself as hyperactive (and still is). Before he had left school he was involved in farming and horses and could be described as a real 'grafter'. Before becoming a great trainer, Jack had ambitions of becoming a Champion jockey and he signed up as Charlie

Hall's apprentice. He rode his first winner at Wetherby on the 22nd April 1957, riding *Sarsta Gri* to win the Bilton Hurdle at the generous odds of 10-1. It was somewhat ironic and quite fitting that he should ride his first winner at the Yorkshire course, as it was at Wetherby that he often visited after truanting from school and sneaked into the course after cycling from Leeds.

He rode a total of forty seven winners during his riding career and these cost him 46 fractures, and as he was never going to a Champion jockey he decided to take up training when in 1972 he bought a farm at Cockerham. He and Jo, a former work rider with Pat Taylor at Beverley his wife by that time began the task of turning a farm into a training centre. So successful were they, that by the time he retired in 2000 he had trained over 1600 winners and had the pleasure of providing Lester Piggott with his final winner when he turned out *Palacegate Jack* at Haydock Park, which coincidentally was where he rode his first winner at the age of twelve.

Jack now lives back in Yorkshire and is the Vice President of the Injured Jockeys Fund and this year 2014 he hopes that his dream of an 'Oaksey House' for the north of England will be finally built at Malton in North Yorkshire. The building to be known as "The House that Jack Built" is on the land that has been purchased from the Fitzwilliam Trust and will be sited on land adjacent to the Malton & Norton Rugby Club. The project is likely to cost in excess of £3m and will provide a fitness centre, respite accommodation, specialist physiotherapy, medical consultations and rehabilitation gymnasiums.

ROYAL VISITORS

Her Majesty the Queen last visited Beverley Racecourse in July 2002. She was a spectator when the Champagne Victor Queens Jubilee Handicap Stakes for Lady Jockeys took place. The race was won by the north's leading amateur jockey Serena Brotherton daughter of David Brotherton the former Steward at Beverley and York who was also a Member of the Jockey Club. Serena rode the Richard Fahey trained *King's Crest,* the winning rider received a gold brooch from the Queen after the race.

In August 1989 Princess Anne rode in the Contrac Computor Supplies Ladies Handicap, she dead heated for second place on *Tender Type,* beaten a short head behind *Waterloo Park* ridden by an 18 year old Clare Balding.

In July 1991 she gained her revenge when in a similar race at Beverley she rode the Richard Whittaker trained *Croft Valley* to victory, beating *Knock Knock,* ridden by Clare Balding by a neck.

The Princess Royal heading to the paddock at Beverley before riding Croft Valley on 15th July 1991.

PRESENT DAY RACECOURSES IN YORKSHIRE AND OTHER'S NOW DEFUNCT

CATTERICK

The first recorded meeting took place on the 22nd April 1783 and for over a century, admission to the course was free and the races were either for private side stakes or for prizes in kind, normally of an alcoholic nature.

For many years the course had no grandstand that is until 1906 which saw its first stand erected. In 1923 a Race Company was formed, but did little to attract either customers or decent class horses.

The turning point in the courses fortunes possible came when Major Leslie Petch became Clerk of the Course; he set about re-designing the track and to improve conditions for both horse and man. He was later succeeded by his nephew, John Sanderson. Today the racing is not of the quality of York or Ascot, but does provide an important venue for both jump and flat trainers, it also provides decent going for the horses.

DONCASTER

Racing is thought to have taken place on the Town Moor, Doncaster before 1600. From the outset the

Mayor and Corporation took great exception to this new recreational pastime, on the grounds that it encouraged many quarrels, murders, and bloodshed by those attending these events, so they ordered that they be prohibited. The ban, happily was not for long, and the Corporation have been major players in the development of the racecourse for many years.

In 1778, the St Leger, the world's oldest Classic horse race, and named after Colonel St Leger, was moved from the original site at nearby Cantley Hall, to the Town Moor. The Town Moor has been the home to this historical race ever since, that is, apart from wartime substitute races. The race was originally run over a distance of 2 miles, which was later reduced in 1813 to one mile, six furlongs and one hundred and ninety three yards. Thirteen years later, the distance was reduced yet again by sixty one yards and finally in 1970 to its present distance of one mile six furlongs and one hundred and twenty seven yards.

A remarkable performance came in the 1822 St Leger when the first four horses to finish were all trained at the historic stable Glasgow House at Middleham, now the home of Chris Fairhurst who succeeded his father Tommy 'Squeak' Fairhurst in 1994. A plaque commemorating the feat can still be seen on the house wall of Glasgow House. The winner was *Theodore* ridden by John Jackson trained by James Croft and owned by Edward Petre, the odds of 100-1 reflected the confidence in the horses chance.

PONTEFRACT

Racing had taken place during the time when Cromwell's men were busy demolishing the Pontefract Castle, but it was to be ninety years later before the Racing Calendar of 1738 was able to record another meeting.

In 1816 the Hon. Edward Petre, inherited nearby Stapleton Hall with a fortune to match. He decided to organize a spring meeting on the Pontefract course. By 1834 the Hon. Edward Petre was broke, losing a fortune by gambling, so without his patronage, Pontefract went into decline and racing ceased in 1835.

In 1852 racing resumed, but the sport was only moderate, however the Corporation acquired the land in 1906, but were reluctant to improve either the racing or the amenities. In any event the First World War intervened and it was not until 1919 that new stands were built. Since that time prize money has increased and the course attracts not only plenty of runners but also plenty of customers. The course itself is believed to be one of the longest in Europe.

REDCAR

Redcar is in the Ceremonial County of North Yorkshire, and racing at Redcar originally took place on the sands, before moving inland in 1872, when at that time the Redcar Race Company was formed. National Hunt racing also took place, but this was soon terminated after only a short time. Apparently this was in 1878 when one day's particular fixture was spoiled by small fields and fighting jockeys. The course attracted top jockeys like Fred Archer, George Fordham and Jack Watts who quite often made the arduous journey from Newmarket.

The course shares with Newmarket the distinction of being the two tracks in Great Britain with a straight one mile, one furlong straight course. It is also worth noting, that like many other northern racecourses, the catering was carried out by Mr P. T. Fawcett, of the 'Red Lion' Inn, South Stainley. His name was synonymous with excellent food and his name will long be remembered by many elderly readers. Another name that many will recall was the Club Secretary, Major J. Fairfax-Blakeborough, he resided at nearby Castleton and was a prolific writer of so many racing books and articles on the Sport of the Kings.

In 1946 Major Leslie Petch became the Managing Director and Clerk of the Course. The Major who had been seen to be a great administrator at York and Catterick, really put Redcar on the racing map. He attracted sponsors, provided better facility's for the race-goer He raised the level of prize money and generally it was a much better place to visit for everyone. In 1964 a new grandstand was opened and since that time a new stable block, lad's hostel and other major improvements have taken place.

RIPON

Bondgate Green was believed to be the first venue for horse racing at Ripon, and that was back in 1664. Since that time, the course has been moved on at least five occasions that is until in 1900 racing was finally established on its present site. It originally provided both flat and National Hunt racing, however within a short space of time 'jump' racing was dropped and the course provided facility's for flat racing. Now known as the 'Garden Racecourse', it provides good facility's and attracts many good class horses, particularly in the Ripon Rowell's Handicap and one of the great sprint races of the racing season, the Great St Wilfred Handicap.

THIRSK

Racing at the present day track began on March 15th 1855 and until 1859 there were hurdle and hunter races on the programme. From the early 1870's into the 1880's almost half the programme was National Hunt racing, however 1889 saw the demise of National Hunt racing and racing was confined to the flat. Racing at Thirsk came about, when in 1854 a local landowner, Squire Frederick Bell of Thirsk Hall, whilst enjoying a convivial evening with friends, decided to stage a race meeting on his estate. Prior to that date racing took place on the Hambleton Hills some eight miles from Thirsk.

For the first twenty years the racing was run by a local Committee and the Clerk of the Course was a local schoolmaster called George Nicholson. The race days were run by amateurs for just the sport, even the Clerk of the Scales weighed the jockeys with a gadget intended to guage the poundage of potato sacks.

However in 1875 the running of the course was taken over by Mr T.S Dawson, one of the then famous training family. He became a real Clerk of the Course and immediately increased the prize mony, for one race he offered a £300 prize fund, it soon became a very popular course and he attracted runners from all over Yorkshire and beyond. Racing prospered until 1914, when after the war, the buildings became dilapidated and the course deteriorated. As a result the course closed for ten years, until Brigadier General Sir Loftus Bates, who had carried out similar work at Pontefract and Hamilton Park, restored the track and racing resumed on the 8th August 1924.

In 1933 all roads led to Thirsk when racing fans from all over the north filled the town to capacity, trains buses and all kinds of motor vehicles arrived in the town on November 3rd. The reason for this congestion was down to one man, Gordon Richards, who much later became the first and only jockey ever, to be Knighted for his services to the Sport of Kings. He was hoping that his mounts at Thirsk that day would provide him with one winner to equal Fred Archer's 1885 record of having ridden 246 winners in a season. Unfortunately for Gordon and all his fans he left Thirsk without riding a winner. However the following day at Hurst Park he beat Fred Archer's record.

In 1940, the town was once again inundated with racing fans when Gordon Richards rode the winner of the substitute St Leger, called the Yorkshire St Leger, when he rode the H.H. Aga Khan's 4-1 chance *Turkham* to win the race.

WETHERBY

The North bank of the River Wharfe is steeped

in horse racing history and it is here that the Romans began the Wetherby story, racing Arab horses at a place called Netherby, just a few miles from Wetherby.

The modern form of racing originally took place on Scaur Bank and moved in 1891 to a new site situated off the York Road which has been used for jump racing ever since. In the 1930's the first terraces were erected, and in the 1970's a new stand joined the two together, a new Millenium stand was opened in 1999, and other major improvements have been made for the jockeys, owners, and trainers. Wetherby remained the sole course in Yorkshire catering just for the National Hunt enthusiast and remains a popular venue with trainers and race-goers. The course has thrived and flourished and became one of the leading National Hunt tracks in the Country.

However the racecourse has been pressing the British Horse Racing Board to hold Flat meetings on the course, this is a project that the Racecourse Management hope will attract new customers to this West Yorkshire Course. As a result, the course was allocated it's first Flat fixture which took place on Sunday April 26th 2015.

YORK

York Corporation is known to have given it's support to horse racing as early as 1530 and, in 1607, racing is known to have taken place on the frozen River Ouse, between Micklegate Tower and Skeldergate Postern.

Whilst there is some uncertainty over when racing first arrived at the present site. The official view is that racing was first held on the Knavesmire in 1730 after being transferred from a site at Clifton Ings, a course which was prone to severe flooding.

However historians believe that a certain Lucius Septimus Severus, Emperor of Rome, provided recreation for the garrison and the rest of his entourage by bringing several teams of Arab horses on an area of York known as the Knavesmire. As a result horse racing, Roman style was staged. The meetings were well supported and betting was very heavy, and as you would expect from the Romans, the racing was governed by strict rules and very professionally organised. So thanks to Severus, who incidentally became the first Roman Emperor to die in Britain, and who was buried at Eboracum, he bequeathed to York a tradition of horse racing that has survived over two thousand years.

York racecourse is renowned for its ability to stage flat racing, and in terms of prize money on offer, it is in the top three racecourses in Britain, and attracts annually over 350.000 race-goers per season. National Hunt racing did take place on the course from 1867 to April 1885, however due to the wet state of the ground, the idea of jump racing was sensibly removed forever.

Racing has not always flourished at the Knavesmire, but under the leadership of administrators like John Orton, R.M James, James Melrose, Leslie Petch and the present Chief Executive and Clerk of the Course, William Derby. The course stage many 'big' races which includes three of the U.K's thirty one Group One races, The International Stakes, the Nunthorpe

Stakes and the Yorkshire Oaks.

Yorkshire at one time, was the hot bed of numerous racecourses and the following places were the home of some form of racing in days gone by. I have listed them alphabetically, I am sure the list is not a comprehensive one, as many farmers allowed their land to be used as and when required:- Bedale: Bradford: Bramham Moor: Burton Constable: Cave (North): Driffield: Egton Bent (Whitby District): Halifax: Harrogate: Helmsley: Holmpton: Kirbymoorside: Leeds: Middleham: Netherby (Nr Harrogate/Wetherby): Northallerton: Nunnington (Nr Helmsley): Ottringham: Owthorpe: Pickering: Robin Hoods Bay (On the sands): Rotherham: Sheffield: Staithes: Stokesley: Tadcaster: Tollerton (Clifford Moor Nr Wetherby): Tunstall: Wath-on-Dearne(Nr Rotherham): The following towns and villages also held race meetings.

BARNSLEY

Races were thought to have been held on Barnsley Moor prior to 1717 and racegoer's attended this meeting before going on to the course at Rotherham.

BOROUGHBRIDGE

Racing was thought to have commenced here prior to 1757 and in 1778 one of the earliest examples of "nobbling" was believed to have taken place on this course. The victim was a five year old mare called *Miss Nightingale,* she was owned by Mr William Bethell of Rise Park. She had carried eight stone when winning a race run in two heats of four miles at York in 1717 and a four mile event at Beverley in June 1778. She was considered one of the best mares of her year and was only beaten twice in her career. She was entered at Boroughbridge in October 1778, but unfortunately she died on the Sunday preceding the race. Suspicion having arisen of her being poisoned, a post mortem on her was ordered, and when cut open, it was soon evident what the problem was. She was found to have about two pounds of duck-shot contained in her stomach. The duck-shot was made up with putty made into balls. In those days Borougbridge had a three day fixture, it was not revealed where *Miss Nightingale* was 'got at' but as her race was not until the Wednesday, it is not likely she would have left Rise by Sunday evening. It was thought that she would have been an easier victim in her home stable than when on her way to Boroughbridge, for it was usual for the lad (s) taking racehorses to meet their engagements to sleep in the box with their charges in hotel yards on the journey to the races.

A Mr William Turner was committed to York Assize Court in 1780 on suspicion of the offence, but was acquitted at the Leeds Assize Court due to the lack of evidence.

BRANDESBURTON

It was reported in the Beverley weekly Recorder and General Advertiser the results of the Brandesburton steeple chasing meeting dated Friday 25th April 1863. It gave no indication where the course was situated, or if it was well attended.

BRIDLINGTON

It will not be widely known that horse racing took place at Bridlington in the mid 1800's. The start being near Sewerby Cliffs and the winning post was located under the Sea Wall Parade. The Boynton family of Burton Agnes were very keen supporters of the venue and Captain George Boynton of Haisthorpe Hall kept a few racehorses at the top of King Street. His stable was later converted to a bank. Pocklington born Jim Snowden was a regular at the meeting. There were only four races at the meeting, chief of which was the Bridlington Quay Handicap, this race was run over a distance of one mile and a quarter. Tommy Ellerington who hailed from Beverley rode all four winners and Tom Green the famous Beverley trainer won two of the events with *Vulcan.*

FILEY

The beach at Filey was yet another venue for horse racing, many holiday makers took to their deck chairs to enjoy the spectacle of horses thundering by whilst the tide was out. It is thought that racing at this location was witnessed as late as the 1920's. Bookmakers were on hand to provide 'punters' with a list of runners and odds.

HARROGATE

A course was laid out on The Stray in 1793, however the first recorded meeting took place in July 1849. However for some reason racing was never popular and it appears by 1855 it had been discontinued forever.

HULL

There was racing in Hull, on a track adjoining Anlaby Road from very early times before moving to Hedon, where the final race took place on the 11th September 1909.

The course at Hedon was formed in 1883 under the name of The East Riding Club and Racecourse Company. Amongst the Directors were The Duke of Hamilton, General Goodlake V.C and Mr H, F. Beaumont. The course at that time covered 267 acres and cost £75.000 to buy and lay out, the work was concluded in 15 months.

However racing only got started there on Friday 24th August 1888. There were three runners in in the Members Plate, two in the selling race, four in the Tranby Croft Hunters Plate, and six in the Asley Handicap, five in in the Burton Constable Stakes and four in the Hedon Plate, a total of twenty four runners. Fields were much the same for the second day's card.

On the first day of the meeting over 14.000 spectators were present which was most surprising as the extra trains that were promised to run from Hull Paragon Station every five minutes failed to materialise.

On the second day, in the presence of Prince Albert Victor (the Duke of Clarence) a crowd of 20.000 attended. It was at this meeting that one of the leading jockeys of the day, John Osborne had a bad accident, apparently about 50 yards from the finish, in the Yarborough Handicap, there was a mounted policeman, whose horse whipped from the rails as the horses were pounding along. *Jessie*, with Osborne up, ran bang into the policeman's horse, and the jockey was thrown to the ground. Osborne was carried to the weighing room, where three doctors attended to him. The doctors quickly diagnosed a dislocated shoulder and the process of re-setting it, was skilfully done.

In 1895, after trying with both flat and jump racing, racing was discontinued. The failure of the course to attract runners and spectators alike was mainly due to the lack transport facilities and the railway company failing to co-operate with the race company in providing an efficient rail service, despite a new rail station being provided next to the course. In 1901 racing was again revived without success and the curtain finally came down on the 11th September 1909.

HUNMANBY

Another favourite course for the Bethell's were they won many races was Squire Humphrey Osbaldeston's course at Hunmanby Hall. The Squire laid out the course in 1772 and hunted many parts of the Holderness area, and also found time to open a sporting club at Driffield. This was the venue at which hunting and racing men gathered. William Bethell's St Leger winner, *Ruler*, won a sweepstake here for three year olds.

In 1782 racing officially ceased and it is recorded that Mr Bethell won the only two races on the card with *Ruler* and *Paymaster*.

KIPLINGCOTES

This East Yorkshire Plate, known as the Kiplingcote's Derby is the oldest endowed race in the world, it is believed, that whilst records show the first running to be in 1619, that it was held some fifty to 100 years prior to that date. The next oldest race, the Newmarket Town Plate was not established until 1666; both races are still held to this day.

The race starts at an old stone post on the grass verge in the parish of Etton and covers a distance of four miles over farm lanes, tracks and grass verges; the winning post is at Londesborough Wold Farm.

The race takes place on the third Thursday in March and one quirk of the ancient rules, means that the second place rider often receives more in prize money than the winner. Another rule states that if the race is not run one year, then the race must never be run again. In the blizzards of 1947 and again in 2001 a sole rider either walked or rode his horse on the course, just to keep the tradition of the race going.

LEEDS

Horse racing took place at more than one location over a number of years in this part of Yorkshire. The first meeting was held in 1682 at Chapeltown Moor, however by 1714 racing was taking place also at Methley Moor. The meetings at Chapeltown Moor were finally ended in 1808. However in 1823 another course was planned, this time by the side of the River Aire, and by the following year, despite great opposition a meeting took place when it was estimated that 100.000 spectators attended. The course was known as Haigh Park Racecourse and a range of stands, constructed of brick and timber were erected.

The course lasted ten years, as in 1833 The Aire & Calder Navigation Company had commenced cutting a new line of river which was to pass through a great part of the course. The promoters decided not to make a new course, due to the considerable expense and no further racing took place.

In 1868 there appears that racing of sorts was taking place on Woodhouse Moor, however it would appear that the Council had not sanctioned the project and racing was soon curtailed.

In 1883 yet another Company was set up to promote racing in the Town, this time on Skelton Moor, but apparently through lack of support the idea was abandoned. Soon after National Hunt racing did take place at Shadwell, but because of lack of entries this project was also abandoned, and racing came to an end in Leeds for ever.

MALTON

Malton is now probably the largest training centre in the north of England and the Langton Wold gallops are used daily by several flat and national hunt trainers.

It is believed that horse racing had been established some time prior to 1692 on the Langton Wolds. However it was not until 1801 that the first grandstand was erected on the land and this was used until 1861 when the final fixture took place.

In 1862 the racecourse was mostly ploughed up, and the grandstand transformed into farm buildings. In 1866 a meeting took place in the Talbot Hotel, Malton, it was convened by a leading trainer of the time, William I'Anson, William had left his native Scotland in 1849 and it was he who was the driving force behind the project. He convinced those that attended a meeting to hold National Hunt racing on the Orchard Fields.

The first meeting took place on the 13th March 1867 and the final meeting was held in 1870. However the persistent William I'Anson laid down a track at Highfield and the first meeting took place there on the 17th March 1882, racing finally ended in 1904 when the racecourse fittings and fixtures were sold off.

ROTHERHAM

Racing commenced at Rotherham on the flat prior to 1727 and came to an end in 1832, however it was not long after that date when jumping took it's place at East Dene. The final meeting at Rotherham was believed to be in the November of 1901.

SCARBOROUGH

Another east coast venue was Scarborough, where in 1751 racing took place on the sands, and on the 12th August Captain Cobourne's black coach gelding, ridden by Captain Jennison Shafto beat Captain Vernon's bay gelding ridden by his owner. The prize was 100 guinnea's

By about 1789 racing officially ended, during the years of racing the Bethell's of Rise had many runners and winners at the seaside venue.

WAKEFIELD

Racing was thought to have taken place on a heath known as Outwood sometime before 1678. It proved a very popular course and within four years the meeting had grown into a fair lasting three days, it was attended by the Duke of Norfolk and many Lords and Knights.

WITHERNSEA

Racing began and ended in the coastal resort of Withernsea in 1857, the fixture attracted plenty of runners and some of the best jockeys attended this inaugural meeting. It is presumed that the primary reason for it's demise, was because of the remote location of this East Riding coastal town.

FLOCKTON GREY

It is doubtful if the Constabulary based in East Yorkshire ever investigated such a complicated fraud as the one involving the grey gelding *Flockton Grey.*

The story unfolded at Leicester racecourse on March 29th 1982 when Kevin Darley rode *Flockton Grey* to win a two year old Auction Stakes by an unbelievable 20 lengths. The Jockey

Club launched an investigation, when it was discovered that across Yorkshire many bets had been struck on the 10-1 winner. It was estimated that the gelding was backed to win £200.000

It was established, with the help of photographs of the winner, taken by a racecourse photographer that the winner was in fact a three year old. It was later concluded, that the horse was in fact, another grey called *Good Hand*. Trainer Nigel Tinkler was so convinced he stated, "If the horse had been pink, I would have still have said it was *Good Hand*, by the horse's expression. I never had any doubt that the winner in the photograph was *Good Hand*". (Nigel Tinkler had trained the horse in 1981).

In 1984, Ken Richardson, Colin Mathison and Peter Boddy appeared at York Crown Court, charged with having conspired to substitute Good Hand for *Flockton Grey*, with the intention of defrauding bookmakers. By a 10-2 majority, the jury found all three defendants guilty.

In 1995, Michael Howard the then Home Secretary, allowed Richardson's request for a judicial review and returned the case to the Court of Appeal. The appeal was heard in December 1996 and Lord Justice Rose, sitting with Mr Justice Keene and Mr Justice Poole, concluded that they did not think the convictions were unsafe and the appeals were dismissed. Richardson received a nine month suspended sentence and fined £20.000 with costs estimated at £25.000, Mattison was fined £3.000 with Boddy receiving a conditional discharge. Kevin Darley was exonerated from having any knowledge of the plot and was never under the slightest suspicion.

OTHER WELL KNOWN JOCKEYS

MARK BIRCH

Mark known to most in the racing world as 'Archie' served most of his apprenticeship with the Newmarket trainer Geoffrey Brooke before transferring his indentures to Peter Easterby in 1968, together they formed a formidable partnership they had a long and successful partnership at Habton Grange. Mark will long be remembered for his association of the legendary horse *Sea Pigeon*, on whom he rode to win two Chester Cup's. During his career he rode over 1500 winners and was crowned "Cock of the North" on numerous occasions. 1968 also saw the start of another long and successful partnership as Mark, met a young lady, Joyce Lynn, who was also working at Habton Grange and who Mark later married. Mark now works for Kevin Ryan and is an invaluable member of his staff. Kevin's stable is also in commuting distance for Mark and Joyce as they are now settled in Malton.

EDGAR BRITT

Edgar Britt born in Australia in 1913 rode his first winner in Sydney in 1930. From 1935 he moved to India, and for a decade, rode for Gaekwar of Baroda as his retained jockey. He moved to Britain to ride for the same owner, whose horses were trained by Sam Armstrong. In 1947 he won the Irish Derby for his boss on *Sayajirao* and on the same horse in the English St Leger. In 1948 he lost the retainer with Gaekwar of Baroda and began riding for Marcus Marsh and Cecil Boyd-Rochfort. He later moved to Yorkshire to ride for Captain Charles Elsey, he and the Captain were successful in all of the English Classic races, except the Derby.

Edgar retired in 1959, and returned to Australia. In 2004 aged 90 years he was awarded the Order of Australia medal, for service to horse racing, as a jockey, commentator, and journalist. He was also inducted into the Australian Racing Hall of Fame, the same year. In 2013 he was interviewed for a racing programme and at the age of 100 looked fantastic.

W.H.CARR

W.H.Carr known to everyone as Harry Carr, had his first ride ever, at Redcar. It was in 1929 at the age of thirteen when he rode *Togo* for his boss, Robert Armstrong of Middleham. The filly was a two year old running in in an all aged selling race, he was led onto the course by his father, who was travelling head lad for Armstrong.

In 1946 he was engaged as first jockey to Captain Boyd-Rochfort.

Who would have thought that this young apprentice, earning just seven-pence a week would eventually become King George VI and Queen Elizabeth II, retained jockey. Harry would go onto ride some exceptional first class horses, and win most of the big races, including Classic races, with the likes of *Meld* and *Parthia*.

In his book, 'Queens Jockey' he nominated a northern trained sprinter as being the fastest horse over five or six furlongs he had ever sat on, that was the Billy Dutton's, *Pappa Fourway*. He described *Alcide* the eight length winner of the St Leger, and *Meld* the winner of the 1000 guineas, Oaks and St Leger as the finest horses he had ridden during a career lasting well over thirty years.

Harry had hoped to retire at the conclusion of the 1964 season, but unfortunately a kidney problem flared up again in June of that year, by July he was obliged to under-go surgery in a London clinic. The surgeon told Harry that it would be best for his health, if he packed up racing straight away. So after thirty three years of race riding, he retired to his farm, a dozen or so, brood mares with their yearlings and foals to keep him and his wife busy.

In 1959 his daughter Anne married Joe Mercer, who incidentally was Harry's best pal in the weighing room.

Harry passed away at the early age of 68.

STEVE CAUTHEN

Steve Cauthen was without doubt one of the finest American jockeys to ride in Brittain. However he and Walter Swinburn did not endear themselves to racegoers at a Beverley meeting on the 7th July 1989. It was the start of a two day meeting and the first day was an evening meeting. Although, present at the meeting, I must rely on the report on the meeting by the Beverley Guardian racing reporter at that time, Max Gambles. He described the start of the meeting as a farce, and strongly critized certain jockeys and local stewards in their behaviour. The first race was due off at 6.45pm and heavy rain began to fall, this effected the course particularly the bottom bend leading to the straight, it also effected the electricity supply as it went off and on periodically. Two of the leading jockeys, namely Steve Cauthen and Wally Swinburn demanded taxi's to Brough airfield, their wishes were granted and they left the course soon after. The stewards delayed the start of the second race, scheduled for 7.10pm and inspected the safety of the track, checking the bend to the straight. The jockeys decided it was not fit and they returned to the paddock refusing to race. At that point several trainers and jockeys drove down the course and by now it was almost 7.45pm, an hour after the first race and the 6.000 paying public were left in ignorance such was the lack of information.

The Bookies had marked up prices, but rubbed them out and they expected the meeting to be cancelled. Thirty minutes later, the crowd were told that racing would go ahead, however many of the spectators had gone home, wet and angry for being left in the dark as to why there were huge delays. John Lowe and another eight riders were reported to the Jockey Club. John Lowe stated, "there was no motive for our action other than believing the ground to be un-safe". He was later summoned to appear before the Stewards at the next meeting on July 18th, to explain his riding in the final two races. The 7.10pm finally went off at 8.28pm amid a shambles of non-runners and the winner *Blakesware Gold* was declared a non-runner only minutes before the off. After the third race, the rest of the card was thankfully abandoned. The following days meeting went ahead as planned, Jimmy Bleasdale won the opener on *Heslington Boy* a selling plater. Later on in the card in the Beverley Amateur Riders Stakes a certain Clare Balding rode *Norquay* trained by her father Ian Balding to victory.

LINDSAY CHARNOCK

One of the north's journeyman jockeys, hardly the best description of one of Yorkshire's most fearless riders. Lindsay proved that on the big occasion, he was more than capable of riding successfully against top class opposition. He won the Cesarewitch on two occasions for Mary Reveley riding *Old Red* to victory in 1995 at 11-1 carrying 7 stone 11 pounds and in 1997 he was again victorious on *Turnpole* at odds of 16-1 carrying one pound less than *Old Red*. He later rode the winners of the Ayr Gold Cup, Lowther Stakes, Windsor Castle Stakes and many more. Lindsay set off on his apprenticeship with Ron Barnes and later transferred to Denys Smith, he rode his first winner at the now defunct racecourse of Lanark, in Scotland in 1971. He was forced to retire from the saddle in 1999 due to circulation problems after riding about 800 winners at home and abroad. In 1987 even Jimmy Fitzgerald entrusted him in the Pitmans Derby the Northumberland Plate, when riding at 7 stone 7 pounds he rode *Treasure Hunter* to victory.

I was once on the gallops at Malton and Lindsay was riding one of Maurice Camacho's 2 year olds who was particularly skittish that morning. As Maurice legged Lindsay up, he retired to see him set off up the gallops and remarked that man had the courage of a lion, and he would never let any horse get the better of him.

Lindsay sadly passed away in August 2015 at the age of 60 years.

PETER CONCANNON

Peter was in Beverley when Brian Henry was in his prime and was an apprentice with 'Snowy' Gray at his York Road stables. He was given many opportunities by 'Snowy' and he must have had around sixty mounts before recording his first victory. He later moved to Malton after 'Snowy' retired and the last his pal of yesteryear Alan English last heard of him, he had taken up singing and he apparently had a good singing voice.

BRIAN CONNORTON

Brian Connorton served some of his time as an apprentice at Norman Bertie's stable at Newmarket before moving to Beverley after transferring his indentures, firstly to Peter Ward who was tragically killed in a motoring accident, and then to 'Snowy' Gray.

He rode his first winner on *Betsy May* on the 15th September 1953. He remained with Snowy for the rest of his career and rode in many big races possible the fastest horse he rode was *Cheb's*

Lad who won the Group 2 Champagne Stakes. However he rated *Lucky Brief* the best, which he rode to victory in the 1962 Dante Stakes at York. He rode over 600 winners before a serious leg injury forced his premature retirement in 1976.

The year before Brian retired, he rode at Newmarket on the 1st of May, when he and other jockeys were abused and threatened by striking stable staff, he described the scenes as disgraceful, adding I don't deny them the right to strike, but to imperil horse and rider as they go down to the start is a totally different matter. As the Pickets stretched out across the course, Brian who was riding one for Geoff Toft called *Cave Warrior*, noticed that Lester Piggott had got through and he went for the weakest part of the line. Charlie Buckton an East Yorkshire farmer and breeder, also had a runner in the race *Dutch Gold* which was ridden that day by Tommy Walsh a young apprentice and they both managed to get to the other side. Tommy came in third at 20-1 and Brian was unplaced but ran a decent race to finish within six lengths of the winner.

Brian's son Nicky also became a jockey and served his time with the Yorkshire based trainer, Bill Watts. He rode his first winner in 1979 and rode for many years in Singapore and India, where he rode most of the 'big' race winners. He also had spells with Maurice Camacho, the former Malton trainer.

STEPHEN (STEVE) DONOGHUE

If the 1901 census had been two years earlier Steve Donoghue may have spent his career in

Yorkshire. However I am ahead of myself by a few years.

Steve Donoghue became one of the best jockeys to have ridden in this Country, and was certainly on a par with Fred Archer, Sir Gordon Richards and Lester Piggott. As a teenager he left home to join John Porter at Kingsclere, however after a mishap on the gallops he soon returned home to Warrington. Whilst at home he was confronted by a local bully and in the ensuing fight, the bully fell heavily on the ground. He sustained a serious injury and Steve thought he was dead, so Steve and his brother George decided to run away. They crossed the Pennines into Yorkshire, and ended up at the stables of Dobson Peacock at Middleham. They were both offered employment, but because of the incident back home, decided to use the surname Smith, instead of their real name. They soon settled in to the daily routine and were both happy in Yorkshire. However officials carrying out work for the 1901 census arrived at the stables, this worried both lads and they decided to run away in case their real identities were revealed.

They eventually finished up in Newmarket, and for the first time they were parted, as they found work at different stables.

Stephen, however didn't remain in Newmarket for long and went over to France to work in a stable in Chantilly. He had his first ever ride in public in France in 1904, finishing third. It was not long after, he had a disagreement with the trainer, and moved to Marseilles and began to ride for a trainer called John Moore. On the 24th of April 1905 he rode his first ever winner.

In 1906, he returned home to England, and later went over to Ireland to sort out problems for his brother George, who had moved there. Steve enjoyed the Irish way of living, decided to stay, and took up an offer to ride there, and soon became a much sought after light weight jockey.

By the end of 1908, he had married an Irish girl, Brigid Behan and the wedding reception was held at the Railway Hotel, Kildare.

At the Liverpool Spring Meeting of 1909, Steve rode his first winner in England, scoring on *Golden Rod* a useful Irish three year old. He then began to ride in England more frequently. By 1911, he had moved over to England, in order to take up a retainer with the trainer Henry Seymour Persse, known to everyone as 'Atty' Persse.

So started a glittering career which before ending he had ridden the Derby winner on six occasions and had been Champion Jockey on ten occasions. He had won the Triple Crown twice and had ridden the winner of every Classic Race.

In the November, of 1917, the year he rode *Gay Crusador* to win the Epsom Derby, Steve was granted a decree nisi dissolving his marriage, on the grounds of his wife Brigid's misconduct with George Walsh, a former jockey and stableman. On St Patrick's Day, the 17th March 1929, he secretly married Ethel Finn an American dancer. In 1938 they parted, and, in 1942 she died after taking an overdose of sleeping tablets.

In 1929 he rode *Brown Jack* to win his first Queen Alexandra Stakes, Steve and the gelding went on to win the same race for the next five years to become the most successful horse in the history of the race.

Steve retired from riding in 1937 and unfortunately suffered a fatal heart attack in 1945 at the age of 60 years.

ALEX GREAVES

Alex Greaves rode mainly in the north and began her career as an amateur rider with David Barron. She rode her first ever winner at Southwell, and rode this track better than most jockeys. During her career she rode over 300 winners, and in 1996 she had the honour of becoming the first ever female jockey to take a ride in the Epsom Derby. The following year she achieved, what was for her, probable the greatest day in her racing life, she rode *Ya Malak* for her husband David, to a dead heat in the Group One Nunthorpe Stakes at York. She also took the honour of Lady Jockey of the Year at the Annual Lester's Awards, on no less than five occasions.

PAUL HANAGAN

Paul was born in Warrington, Cheshire in 1980, however his progress as a jockey was as a result of strong links with Yorkshire, and Malton is where he really learned his trade. As a youngster his ambition was to be a professional footballer, however with his stature that was never going to happen. Today he follows Liverpool and always watches out for their results. His father Geoff was riding work for trainer Terry Caldwell, and Paul decided that because of his size to give it a go, even agreeing to spending time on a work experience scheme with him. He then embarked on a nine week course at the British Racing School in 1997. Following that, he moved to Yorkshire and spent some time with Malcolm Jefferson, who was better known as a trainer of National Hunt horses. However it was Malcolm who gave Paul his first ride at Haydock Park on the 4th September 1998, and he managed a respectable fourth place on *Stone Beck*.

The following year on Mr Jefferson's recommendation that he should join a flat yard, he joined Richard Fahey stable in Malton as an apprentice jockey. In 1999 he managed to ride six winners, not bad for a young man who had only sat on a horse just five years previously. By the year 2000 he had become champion apprentice with eighty seven winners under his belt. Two years later he won the John Smith's Cup at York on *Vintage Premium* trained by his boss Mr Fahey, who was heard to say "If this boy is not champion jockey one day, I will give up the game". As predicted by his great mentor, Paul became champion jockey in 2010 and again in 2011, thus becoming the first northern based jockey ever to win the championship more than once. The future became even brighter for this quietly spoken and unassuming young man, when in 2012 he was appointed first jockey to the Deputy Ruler of Dubai Hamdan bin Rashid Maktoun, after the retirement from the saddle of Richard Hills. He achieved an ambition to ride a Classic winner, when riding the John Gosden trained and Hamdan bin Rashid Maktoun owned winner of the 2014 Oaks at Epsom, on the very impressive *Taghrooda*.

BRIAN HENRY

Brian arrived in Beverley to become an apprentice with Pat Taylor and they immediately struck up a wonderful partnership. So much so, that in 1959 he almost won the Apprentice Championship, Bobby Elliot beating him on the last day of the season by one winner. However the following season saw Brian gain his revenge when beating Elliot in the Championship. In July of that season

Reppin Castle trained at Beverely by Alf Smith and ridden by Brian Henry winning the John Hudson Memorial Handicap at Beverley in 1978

Brian must have made some sort of record when riding *Airdale* to victory at Catterick, on that day he had ridden the 41st winner of his career and all these victories had come against senior jockeys, not bad for a young jockey born in the tiny village of Withnell near Chorley in Lancashire.

EDWARD HIDE

Edward Hide, who for many years rode for Captain Elsey at Malton. Edward was a great rider, and was unfortunate never to be the winner of the Jockeys championship table. He came second on one occasion, however numerically his best season came in 1994 when he rode 137 winners, during his glorious career he rode 2.593 winners.

That total, included six Classic winners, the first being in 1959 when he rode *Cantelo* to win the St Leger for Captain Elsey, the filly was owned by the bookmaker William Hill. He followed this up in 1978 when riding *Julio Mariner*, trained by Clive Brittain to win the same race. Between those dates, Edward rode *Pia*, again for Captain Elsey to win the 1967 Oaks at Epsom. This was followed by two victories in the 1000 guineas, in 1972 riding for trainer "Bill" Watts he won on *Waterloo*, and followed this up by winning the 1977 event for the Yorkshire stable of Mick Easterby on *Mrs McArdy*.

In the 1973 Derby he agreed to ride *Morston* for trainer Arthur Budgett, *Morston* never ran as a two year old, making his racecourse debut in a Maiden at Lingfield Park, where he won well, but ran rather green. For the Derby he was priced at

25-1, which possible summed up his chances of winning. However Arthur Budgett, who owned the colt had complete faith in him, and his faith was not misplaced when *Morston* won by a half a length from Cavo Doro. *Morston* never ran again, as he sustained a tendon injury when being prepared for a big race at York, and was retired from racing.

JOE MERCER

Joe who was born in Bradford in 1934, six years after his brother Emmanuel Lionel "Manny", who was a brilliant jockey but was killed on the way to the start of a race at Ascot in 1959 when riding *Priddy Maid*. "Manny" had already won two Classic's and other 'big' races, including the Washington D.C International in 1952 at the age of 24 years. He is buried in Newmarket Cemetery.

Joe and "Manny" were part of a family of eight and Mr Mercer Senior was an accomplished coach/car painter. For some reason Joe wanted to follow his brother into horse racing and started life at Major Fred Sneyd's stable at Sparsholt, Berkshire, where he spent, at the age of twelve years of age, his school holidays riding out and mucking out the stables. He later became the Major's apprentice and rode his first winner on *Eldoret* at Bath in 1950. He was later to become the Champion Apprentice in 1953, the same season saw him ride his first Classic winner on *Ambiguity*. He later transferred his indentures to Jack Colling at West Isley. During his career he will be forever be remembered for his riding of *Brigadier General*. Whilst a Beverley horse will also be remembered by Joe. The Geoff Toft trained *Gunner B* who Joe rode to win on more than one occasion. However the owner moved the horse from Geoff in 1978 to the stable of Henry Cecil where Joe was the stable jockey he then won the Eclipse Stakes among others. I devoted a paragraph on Gunner B within this book. Joe rode his last winner on *Bold Rex* at Doncaster in 1985 and by that time he had ridden over 2.800 winners in Britain. After his retirement he worked initially as a Jockey's Agent before becoming Racing Manager for Maktoum Al Maktoum.

BRIAN LEE

Brian was another fine jockey in the early 1960's. He was born in Halifax, Yorkshire and whilst he was Ernie Davey's main stable jockey, Major Holliday a Yorkshire based owner/breeder recognised Brian's talent and offered him in 1960 a retainer to ride his horses that were due to carry a light weight.

Brian rode his very first winner at Beverley in 1959 on *Game Star*.

BILLY NEVETT

Billy Nevett was born in Lancashire, but lived in Yorkshire for most of racing life. He was affectionately named the 'Cock of the North' due entirely to the number of times he was the leading rider in the North of England. Billy rode a total of 2.068 winners, which included three wartime Derby winners, from 1940 to 1945, the worlds greatest race was transferred to Newmarket, and Billy rode the winners of three of the five races, in

1941 he rode *Owen Tudor* for Fred Darling. Then in 1944 he rode *Ocean Swell* for Jack Jarvis and the following year succeeded on the fabulous *Dante* for Mathew Peacock. Billy rode winners at Ripon, where the Billy Nevett Memorial Handicap commemorates his many course achievements.

Mention of *Dante*, reminds me of an unusual incident that was recorded whilst *Dante* was having a gallop at Middleham before the Derby. A stone flew up and struck him in the eye, it was thought that the injury may blind him for life. His owner Sir Eric Ohlson called upon a Harley Street eye specialist, a certain Williamson Noble to travel to Middleham to examine the horse. Mr Noble was the oculist responsible for looking after the eyesight of none other than Winston Churchill. An operation was performed by Mr Noble, the first ever time he had ever operated on a horse, and told the delighted owner that there would be no charge for his work, unless the horse won the Derby. Apparently after his Derby win, Mr Noble received a very substantial reward for all his work on the horse, he also tipped off Sir Winston that Dante would win the Derby which ensured that his reputation would be enhanced, particularly in Downing Street. But although the work carried out by Mr Noble ensured he was fit to run in the Derby, it was later found that his eye problem was not an injury caused by a stone, but the early stages of a generative disease which eventually blinded him.

JOHNNY SEAGRAVE

Johnny Seagrave served his apprenticeship with trainers Billy Smallwood and Ernie Davey at

Malton, from 1947 to 1955. It was at Lincoln in 1948 that he rode his very first winner. However it was not until the 1970's that trainers began to recognise how good a rider Johnny was. He began to ride good horses for the likes of Rufus Beasley, Pat Rohan and Bill Elsey. This is highlighted by the number of winners he rode in his first 17 years as a jockey, which totalled 81, compared to the last 19 years, when he was successful on 849 occasions. His career came to a premature end, when after a particularly painful fall, he was obliged to undergo an examination by a Jockey Club appointed doctor. The doctor warned Johnny that if he continued to ride, and had further falls, they could prove fatal, and was advised to retire. This advice he reluctantly took and embarked on a totally new career, that of training and breeding greyhounds. He became very successful and had many winners at the Craven Park Track at Hull.

JOE SIME

Joe was born in Liverpool in 1923 but spent nearly the whole of riding career in Yorkshire after serving his apprenticeship with Dawson Waugh at Newmarket and riding his first winner on *Firle* at Newmarket in 1941. He was also the Champion Apprentice in 1943, 1944 and in 1946 when he rode 40 winners. Joe, however will always remembered for his association with the Sam Hall stable at Middleham. Joe was always able to ride at a weight of under 8 stone and big handicaps came their way at regular intervals including the Ebor Handicap on four occasions. In 1967 at Beverley, not many race-goers who were present would have believed that an unplaced horse ridden by Joe Sime would become a Grand National hero, winning the race a record breaking three times, *Red Rum* was that horse, and he ran in a five furlong event at Beverley. He also rode winners at the Royal Ascot meeting, including the Royal Hunt Cup and Wokingham Handicap. One of Joe's great achievments was to win the Great Metroplitan Handicap for her Majesty the Queen on *Gold Aura*.

SIMON WALKER

Simon Walker is recognised as one the best amateur jockey's, if not the best amateur riding today. Simon began riding out at his father Tony's Church Farm, Etton, near Beverley, Tony trained Point to Pointer's as well as running a successful livery yard. It was here that Simon and his brother Robert excelled as youngster's in competitions confined to Shetland ponies. The pair of them even rode out with the Holderness Hunt. Simon now in his mid thirty's has ridden over 50 winners under rules, over 80 point to point winners and over 400 winners of Arab races, he is associated with Bill Smith the trainer of pure bred Arab horses.

ROBERT WINSTON

Robert is no Yorkshire man, having been born in the Ballymun area of Dublin. He could ride bare back on horses through the streets of Dublin from a very early age, so it was no surprise that he would eventually become a jockey. He chose Yorkshire as his base. So, it was in 1995 at the tender age of sixteen and never having been away from his family before, he arrived at the stable of Richard Fahey. Robert coming from a part of Dublin, that could only be described as a difficult area to grow up in, it was I suppose that during his formative years, as a jockey it was inevitable he had his problems with the various Authority's. However despite various set backs he remained very positive, and always looked forward to further successes. He will always remember his first winning ride, when beating his fellow Irish man Pat Eddery in a finish. And in 1999 he became Champion Apprentice jockey riding 49 winners. It was about this time that he moved stables to Linda Ramsden's.

In 2005 he was favourite to win the Jockeys Championship when well ahead of the second place jockey and eventual winner Jamie Spencer. That was until he was badly injured when his mount *Pearls a Singer* trained at Newmarket by Michael Bell, slipped at the home bend and crashed through the rails at Ayr. Robert sustained very serious injuries and had a total of six plates inserted in his face during his four months out of action. When recalling the fall to me, he clearly remembered the start of the race, whilst waiting for the rest of the field to enter the stalls. He found a money spider crawling along his sleeve, he removed it and placed it on the frame work of the stalls. Though not superstitious, he has often reflected on the situation, should he have removed the spider or left it on his sleeve.

The following season he was also in a promising position in the Jockeys table when a ban cost him all chance he had. He still harbours ambitions to take the Championship, but feels that to have any real chance a jockey must have the backing of a really big stable. However in the 2006 season he did achieve a life times ambition to ride in the Epsom Derby when riding *Papal Bull* for trainer Sir Michael Stoute, the colt finished a respectable 10th of the 18 runners, beaten about nine lengths

He rates York as his favourite track in Yorkshire, not surprisingly as he has ridden big race winners there, one in particular *Caspar Netsher,* winning the 2011 Historic Gimcrack Stakes.

OWNERS and OFFICIALS

LURLINE BROTHERTON

Mrs Brotherton lived near Malton and was persuaded to go into racehorse ownership by her husband. When she finally retired from owning horses she had amassed over 300 winners both on the flat and over the jumps. Her most famous victory without doubt would be the 1950 Grand National winner *Freebooter* a 10-1 chance, who was ridden to victory by Jimmy Power and trained at Ripon by Mr Robert (Bobby) Renton. Her jockeys also included Tim Molony, Brian Marshall, Johnny East, Terry Biddlecombe, Stan Hayhurst, Josh and Macer Gifford, David Mould, Brian Fletcher, Barry Brogan and Jack Berry. On the flat they included amongst others, Doug Smith, Lester Piggott, Eddie Hide, Sandy Barclay, Eddie Larkin, Billy Nevett, and D. W. Morris. Her main trainer over the jumps was Robert Renton who believe it or not was still riding out and training horses at the age of 83 years. In the 1960's he surely would have created some sort of record if it had not been for the very firm ground at Hexham. At the age of 74 years he was down to ride *Devon Peter* but because of the state of the ground and should the horse have taken a tumble he would have been badly injured, so he passed the mount to Johnny East. The horse did fall at the third fence and Johnny received severe bruising, however his mount *Devon Peter* escaped without injury. Her other trainers included, Tommy Shedden, Arthur Thomas, Mick Easterby and Jimmy Fitzgerald.

Horse Racing is governed by lot's of hindsight and I suppose everyone can re-call the exploits of the famous *Red Rum* in the Grand National, many will re-call that *Red Rum* was once owned by Mrs Brotherton, and a former famous jockey Tim Molony, it was he who had originally purchased *Red Rum* for a paltry 400 guineas before he was switched to the ownership of Mrs Brotherton, which resulted in him winning hurdle races and five steeplechases for her. However he did suffer with a bone disease called Pedalostitis, which meant many expensive visit's to the Vet's, so it was decided to enter him at the August Doncaster bloodstock sales. And as they say the rest is history, as eight months later he was winning the Grand National for the first time for new owner Noel le Mare and trainer Ginger McCain. You may recall that that Ginger trained near the sea, so the horse spent lot's of time walking and running in the sea water, which had certainly helped his medical problem.

It may be of interest to the reader that *Red Rum* ran at Beverley as a two year old and finished unplaced.

LORD and LADY MANTON.

The East Riding of Yorkshire was home,to one of the most successful Senior Steward's the Jockey Club has ever known, in Lord Manton. He was without doubt a round peg in a round hole, which, as many of you will appreciate, has not always been the case with these sort of appointments. Before taking over the peerage, on the death of his father in 1968, he was known as Rupert Watson, and like his father before him, rode successfully under National Hunt Rules. in fact he was known to be a fearless amateur rider who rode well over 100 winners. Without doubt the highlight of his career was when he rode *Gay Monarch* to victory in the 1955 Kim Muir at the Cheltenham Festival. Apart from his experience as a jockey, he was a member of the Horserace Betting Levy Board, Chairman of York Race Committee, a Member of the Tattersall's Committee, which ruled on betting disputes, a Director of Thirsk Racecourse and a Steward at Beverley, York, and Doncaster racecourses. During his spell as Senior Steward he liased with prominent members of the Conservative Government to implement new legislation both on course and off course for the good of racing. Indeed he was responsible fo the implementation of plastic running rails that replaced those fearful concrete posts seen on most racecourses. These are quite clearly shown on the photograph at Beverley when Brian Connorton was beaten into second place by the South African rider John Gorton seen on the following page.

As an owner/breeder he also enjoyed great success, and one of his home breds to give him much satisfaction was after his son Miles rode *Silver Stick* to win the 1998 running of the Military Gold

John Gorton rides Expo to win at Beverley beating Brian Connorton riding Mautessa owned by Mine Host of the Green Dragon Public House. (Please note the lethal concrete posts that Lord Manton fought so fiercely to have removed from all racecourses.

Cup at Sandown Park. At the presentation he was heard to say to the Queen Mother, "I saddled the horse, I bred the horse and the jockey". Away from the racecourse he loved his hunting and shooting and was a renown Bridge player. Lady Manton was also a lover of horse racing and often attended meetings, particular in Yorkshire, she was also an owner. She now lives quietly in Leicestershire having lost her husband in 2003.

JOURNALISTS and COMMENTATORS

MALCOLM TOMLINSON

Malcolm was born and bred in Beverley and still lives in the area. His late father was a watch and clock repairer and worked at his shop in the town centre, a shop which incidentally is still there today and still run by a member of the family, Malcolm's brother. As a clock repairer Malcolm's father was responsible for maintaining the clocks that were dotted about the Beverley racecourse, so it was inevitable that Malcolm paid many visits to course at an early age. However on leaving school, horse racing was not on Malcolm's agenda and he obtained his BA (Hons) degree in Drama and English, he later trained at Mountview Theatre School in London. He later appeared in several of the leading television soap opera's, including Emmerdale, Hollyoaks and Eastenders. He has also appeared in numerous other television plays and films.

Apart from being an Actor, he took up as a race course commentator and quickly gained a reputation as being one of the best around and lead him to becoming one of a team of twenty commentators who cover the whole of the racecourses in the United Kingdom. He has commentated as far north as Perth in Scotland and as far south as Goodwood in Sussex. He can often be found commentating at his home track of Beverley where he has become a firm favourite with not only the management team but also with the racegoer who find his clear and precise commentary pleasing to the ear.

JOHN SEXTON

I have known John for many years, as he lived a couple of miles down the road from me. He was not a Yorkshireman, but during the early part of his career (some sixteen years) he worked for the Hull Daily Mail, based in Hull. He covered various sports and he reported on the fortunes of Hull Kingston Rovers, he also reported on local greyhound racing, horse racing and many other sports that the Editor called him to cover. In 1982 he was promoted to the Racing Editor, a role he later combined with the Northern Echo. In 1988 he accepted the Racing Editor's post at the Wolverhampton Express and Star Newspaper, he covered the sport nationwide and attended all the major meetings. He was also covering the major races in Ireland, France and the United States of America. In 1995 he covered the Queen Elizabeth II Cup in Kyoto, Japan.

In 1991 he received the greatest honour a horse racing journalist could receive that of Horse Racing Journalist of the Year. The only occasion that a Regional Evening Newspaper scribe has received the award. I was present to see him accept the award and his acceptance speech brought the house down. He was so highly thought of by his colleagues, that in 1994 he was elected as the President of the Horse Writers & Photographers Association. In 2012 he was appointed Chairman of the "Go Racing in Yorkshire and has brought new ideas and initiatives to this prestigious role. John, is now based in Cumbria and is enjoying providing raceday presentations for the picturesque course at Cartmel.

TOM O'RYAN

Tom is the brother of Robin that vastly experienced and so unassuming assistant to the very highly successful trainer Richard Fahey, Tom and Robin came over from Ireland and followed in the footsteps of their father, a brilliant horseman. Tom is now recognised as one of the leading writers in the world of horse racing and another northern based scribe to win the coveted award of Horse Racing Journalist of the year. Tom was previously a jockey and still loves riding out each morning for trainers based in Malton. Tom rode his very first winner in 1972, when he rode *Vivacious Boy* carrying the feather weight of 6 stone 10 pounds.at Beverley to win at odds of 20-1, the winner was trained by that great northern trainer David Chapman, David specialised in buying cheap cast offs by other stables and invariable winning a small race or even the bigger races with the likes of *Chaplin's Club, Glencroft, Soba,* who was originally a selling plater but who went on to win thirteen races including the Stewards Cup, and of course Quito, he was bought out of the Godolphin stable for 3.500 gns and won over £450.00 in prize money. David, sadly, passed away in 2011 and he was succeeded by his talented granddaughter Ruth.

Tom spent sometime in the Intensive car unit at the Hull Royal Infirmary in 2013, when he received serious injuries whilst cutting the grass in his paddock at his home. Happily Tom is back writing for the Racing Post and fronting the camera's for Racing U.K.

JOHN MOONEY

John was born into a family of bookmakers, his Dad and his three brothers were all street 'bookies'. They covered the Hessle Road of Hull, which was an area renowned for the number of men who worked in the fishing Industry, many of these workers found that they had very little time between trips so they enjoyed what little they had to drink and gamble. When betting became legal in 1961, he and members of the family, opened six betting shops. He later joined the old established bookmaking business, and well known in the Hull area, Rossy Brothers. After a time he went into journalism, he worked for various groups, which included Radio Humberside and the Hull Daily Mail. He later moved to Leeds to work for the Press Association, where he became Racing Editorial Manager. One of John's clients was the Yorkshire Post and for several years he covered horse racing under the non-de-plume of 'The Duke'. He is now semi-retired and produces daily previews for BskyB web-sites and occasionally does pieces for the Hull Daily Mail.

Mr J- FAIRFAX -BLAKEBOROUGH

Was a regular and prolific writer of horse racing and country matters and was a regular contributory to the Beverley Guardian. In his column of June 14th 1947, he recalled, that whilst attending Redcar Races he had heard from a former jockey, Jack Anderson that he was about to re-commence race riding after being retired from the saddle for more than twenty years. Jack was born in Kingston-upon-Hull in 1890 and had been assisting Mr Mather a trainer based in Richmond. Before his retirement Jack had served his apprenticeship with Melton Vasey, he had ridden his first winner in 1906 at Catterick at the age of sixteen years. At one time Jack had lived in Beverley. When he decided to resume his riding career, he could still 'do' a handy weight and would be riding for Mr Mather. Incidentally Melton Vasey, Jack's former Master, was the brother of Percy Vasey who was also a trainer of some repute and was based at Wetherby.

TRAINERS - RETIRED

MARY REVELEY

It is always a pleasure to chat with George Reveley, the husband of Mary, and I did so recently, at the only jump course in the East Riding, that is the Point to Point course situated in the grounds of Lord Hotham's home in Dalton Park, near Beverley, which has been so well organised by The Holderness Hunt Committee for fifty years or so.

George, like Mary, is so unassuming, and from starting out with Pointers, becoming a Permit Holder and then progressing to a Dual -Purpose trainer, who would have envisaged this family concern training well over 2.000 winners and still churning winners out today, with son Keith now at the helm. Keith still trains at the Groundhill Stable at Lingdale, near Saltburn in the Ceremonial County of North Yorkshire.

When they started out in the early 1980's the facilities at the farm were not the best, indeed, at one stage they decided to train at the famous Whitewall stables owned by Frank Carr in Malton. The move was not the success they thought it might have been and the decision to return to Groundhill Farm and develop the gallops proved the right thing to do. Whilst Mary held the licence, son Keith proved a very able assistant, son John mainly concentrated on the farm. George described himself as the 'odd job' man and box driver. Later when Keith took over from Mary, it was James, Keith's son who became the jockey to so many of the jump winners, and who also rode regularly for other stables in this Country and in France. When asked for his favourite horse they had trained, George was quick to sing the praises of *Mellottie* the winner of the 1991 Cambridgeshire when ridden by John Lowe at 10-1, and the popular *Cab On Target,* winner of twenty races covering a period of nine years and ridden in thirteen of these successes by one of the finest jump jockeys in the north, Peter Niven. In May 2011 Peter became the first Scotsman and only the sixth ever jockey to ride 1000 winners. Peter is now a trainer at Malton, North Yorkshire.

PETER EASTERBY

Miles Henry "Peter" Easterby was born on the 5th of August 1929. He combined farming with training and started with seven horses at his stables at Habton Grange near Malton in 1950. He had to wait three years to saddle his first winner, when *Double Rose* won a £102 hurdle race at Market Rasen he then had a two year wait to saddle his first Flat race, when *King's Coup* scored at Thirsk at odds of 25-1. By the time he retired in 1996 he had saddled over 1.000 winners in Britain under both codes. He won the Champion Hurdle in 1967 with *Saucy Kit* and the Cheltenham Gold Cup with Alverton in 1979 and *Little Owl* in 1981.

He later trained the brilliant *Sea Pigeon* to win two Champion Hurdles and on the flat the same horse won the Chester Cup twice in 1977 and 1978, Mark Birch the jockey on both occasions the following year *Sea Pigeon* won the Ebor Handicap carrying ten stone and was ridden by Jonjo O'Neil who was a brilliant National Hunt jockey based in the north of England. He also trained *Night Nurse* to win two Champion Hurdle's in the 1976/77 seasons, on both occasions ridden by Paddy Broderick. *Night Nurse* later became a fine steeplechaser and finished second to his stable mate *Little Owl* in the 1981 running of the Chelenham Gold Cup.

When he retired in 1966, his son, Tim took over, and carried on the stables winning ways and won the St Leger in 2002 with *Bollin Eric*. One of his great successes was with Lady Legard's homebred *Somnus.* He was entered for the sales at Doncaster and failed to attract a bid that Lady Legard thought suitable and she put him into training with Tim Easterby, Tim soon decided to have him gelded and he was entered for the big sales races, he went onto to win the Redcar Two-Year -Old Trophy and other sprint races at two and three years old, winning in the region of over three quarters of a million pounds for Lady Legard and her partner in the gelding, Roger Sidebottom, he continued racing until reaching the age of six years old when he was retired in 2008.

HUMOROUS TALES

Whilst racing can be a serious business, it has more than it's share of lighter moments, I am grateful to all those who have contributed to this part of the book. Please enjoy them, they are true.

DALE GIBSON

Dale retired from the saddle in October 2009 after 24 years of race riding. He rode 528 winners during his career, including 5 for Her Majesty the Queen. He now works for the Professional Jockeys' Association as the Industry Liaison Officer.

Dale relates this story. I was riding at Beverley in July 2002, and was approached by the author of this book, Ken, to give a few words of wisdom to a group of racegoer's who were having a taste of the Sport of Kings for the very time. My opening words went something like this, "do not back any of my mounts today, none of them are fancied" No one was more surprised than me, when later that afternoon I finished up riding a treble for Mick Easterby, one of them a 50-1 shot. This particular horse had been running badly and was wearing a visor for the first time.

After the 50-1 shot had returned to the winners enclosure, the Stewards held an enquiry into it's improved form. And of course we were called into the Stewards room, Mick walked in eating an ice cream cornet, he explained to them that he thought they had called him in to congratulate him for saddling a treble at the course. However they wanted to know his explanation for the winners improved form. Thinking quickly, he explained that he was a bit short staffed with summer holidays and he had let his Secretary ride work on it. The Stewards were none the wiser and they agreed that either his Secretary had improved the horse or it had thought it was easier to carry me at only 7stone 12 pounds.

During the enquiry, my eyes could not leave the ice cream Mick was holding and I am sure the Stewards were as equally mesmerised at it could be seen to be slowly melting and running down his hand.

JACK BERRY M.B.E

Jack became an apprentice jockey to Charlie Hall who trained near Wetherby, Yorkshire, and rode his first winner over hurdles in 1957 at the age of 17 years. It gave him great pleasure as was on a 10-1 shot *Sarsta Gri* and was at his local course at Wetherby.

He later took up training and from very humble beginnings, he and his wife Jo turned out over 1600 winners including achieving a life long ambition of training the Ayr Gold Cup winner, with *So Careful* in 1998. Jack who was also renown for his training of 2 year olds. He later retired to live in Yorkshire and is now the Vice President of The Injured Jockeys Fund, and a tireless worker.

Jack relates these stories. In a race at Catterick I had a fall at the second last fence, as I got up, one of the other jockeys, who had fallen at the third last, but re-mounted was hacking back. As I had a ride in the next race, I shouted to him "Give us a lift back" The rider replied, "No problem, Jack, hop on". So, I vaulted up behind him. He was steering and I had my feet in the irons. As we approached the stands, we were going faster and faster., I shouted to him, "Can't you hold him, he's away with us, let me off and stop pratting about", or words to that effect. It looked as though we could do another circuit of the track, so I decided to bail out, and slipped off the horse's back, did six brilliant somersaults and in the process added a few more bruises to my already battered body.

Another time one of my owners and Jo decided to go to Doncaster St Leger Sales, I was going racing, and I warned them only to buy something that was sound. They came back with a leggy, bay filly which had cost 520 guineas, looking at her breeding, I asked them, "What's wrong with her?" "She's a bit straight in front", replied Jo.

When I saw the filly, I said to them, "Were you both drunk, or what"? Anyway Jo took over the ownership of the filly and named her, *I Don't Mind.* Before the Flat season started in March, we took our four two year olds to Carlisle for a gallop. Eric Apter the Beverley based jockey rode our Flat runners when he could, and he rode the filly. She beat the other three out of sight.

We took our time with her and I decided to enter her in a seller at Beverley on the 10th of June. It was an absolute doddle for her and she trotted up, in a time that was on a par with the big two year old race of the day. Her starting price was 4-1 and I had £20 on her.

At the subsequent auction, it was like Doncaster Sales when Henry Beeby is selling a good horse-everybody came to see the action.

"You won't want it back, will yer?" said Mick Easterby. "Yes I will- the missus owns her". "I've a job for it, that's all " Mick went on, "They're a bad lot-mine's ner good, ner good at all " The auctioneer began taking bids from all directions, Mick was breathing down my neck, "Have yer finished ?". I hadn't even started, they were going that fast!. Jo was standing next to me, giving me a real hard time, every time it was my turn to bid, she would say, "*You*, put her in the seller, so you can get her back". I bought her in for 3.700 guineas, which at that time (1976) was a record for Beverley. The Clerk of the Scales gave me a blank cheque, as I didn't have one with me. I put our banks name and address on and signed it, then, next day, I rang our bank manager, "Please honour this cheque until Friday, as I might get warned off if it's not paid". And I reassured him that I'll sell my cattle to pay for her, (which I did).

IAN BALDING

Ian Balding was born in the United States of America on November 7th 1938, and came to England with his family in 1945. His father was a racehorse trainer as was his elder brother Toby. Kingsclere became his home at the age of 26 years and it was here that he earned his reputation as an Internationally respected trainer. He trained mainly on the Flat, but did win the Sun Alliance

Novices' Hurdle in 1991 with *Crystal Spirit.* He won many 'big' races including the Derby and the Prix de l'Arc in 1971 with *Mill Reef.*

On his retirement he was made an Honorary member of the Jockey Club.

In 1970 we brought *Mill Reef* up to York to run in the Gimcrack Stakes. He was a hot favourite, but having walked the course (it had rained all night), I had made up my own mind that it was only barely raceable, and certainly not fit ground to run a really good horse on. I sought out the owner, Mr Mellon who was having lunch with the Chairman and other Directors, I told him how I felt. Seeing the disappointment on his face as it was the first time he had come over from America to see his flying 2 year old run. I told him we could wait until after our jockey Geoff Lewis had ridden in the first race and we would discuss it again before making a final decision.

We had this conference outside the weighing room after the first race, where both trainer and jockey virtually begged Paul Mellon not to run. I will always remember how he said, "I just have this feeling that everything will be o.k, and that we should run, and if anything went wrong, I will take the blame". Well thank God he had come over to see her run and make that important decision, or none of us would have had the privilege of seeing the great horse win by an amazing 10 lengths that day and seemingly never get out of a hack canter!

My other story also concerns a race at York. It was the Musidora Stakes at the May meeting in 1974, and we had the favourite belonging to Her Majesty The Queen called *Escorial* ridden by

Lester Piggott. The Queen herself was there to see her homebred filly run. *Escorial* was a difficult, temperamental, filly but very talented, and at this point she was one of the ante-post favourites for the Oaks. I had warned the Queen that I was worried about the long walk over from the stables and just to be sure she didn't get loose, I had organised for one our lads (who was a good rider) to ride her over with her 'lad' leading her and our travelling head lad walking the other side of her also with a lead on the filly.

I was watching with the Queen up in the Royal Box having rather smugly told her of all these precautions I had taken to ensure she got safely across to the pre-parade ring. Well they all got about half way across when suddenly *Escorial* reared up, and fell over backwards and in doing so managed to get free of all three of my lads! She galloped off to the far end of the course (loose of course) and I quickly excused myself from the Queen - who was not best pleased!- to go and help catch her! By the time I got out to the middle of the course, a Yorkshire trainer (Joe Mulhall) had managed to catch her somewhere down near the 7 furlong start. Happily her excursions must have done her more good than harm, as *Escorial* won the Musidora quite impressively and in the end the Queen was pleased she had come to York. However her temperament got the better of her in the Oaks and ran most disappointingly.

MARK BIRCH

In the 1970's Mark was riding at Pontefract on a fancied horse trained by his Governor Peter Easterby. About a furlong from home Mark found himself without a whip, having dropped it in a skirmish earlier on in the race. Dropping back through the field was a no hoper being ridden by Tony Ives, Mark knowing his mount was on the lazy side and would need the persuader in the closing stages, he asked Tony to pass him his whip, which he kindly did so. As a result of this gesture, Mark scraped home, to the relief of everyone connected to the horse. The Stewards held an inquiry into the events of the race, however as they had not come across such an occurrence before, they let the result stand. For those readers, like myself had often wondered what had happened to Tony Ives, the North Yorkshire born ex-rider who spent most of his apprenticeship with Snowy Wainwright. Mark's wife Joyce, recalls that he his now living in Chiang Rai, in Northern Thailand, with his Thai born second wife and they have three children.

INDEX

Aidan O'Brian 7
Aike Grange Stud 52, 79
Aintree 76
Airdale 121
Alan English 4, 114
Alan Munro 74
Alcide 111
Alexander Gray 26
Alex Greaves 118
Alfred Crosskill 19
Al Maktoum 79, 123
Altisidora 17
Ambiguity 122
American 111, 117
Androma 74
Andy Capp Handicap 87
Apprentice Championship 120

Arab Races 126
Aragon 49
Archbishop Neville 10
Archbishop Wickwane 9
Arthur Budgett 121-122
Ashgill 37
Aske 61
Asley Handicap 102
Atlas 48
Ayr 69, 72, 87, 113, 127, 141

Ballymarais 75
Barefoot 18
Barnsley 99

Barry Brogan 128
Baumber 71
Beckside 27
Belfort 51
Delville 57
Bentley 36
Bernard Shaw 52
Bert Firestone 71
Beverley Guardian 4, 21, 112, 135

Beverley Minster 9
Beverley Race Company 12, 31

Beverley Racecourse 63, 84-85, 90

Beverley Town Council 55
Beverley Weekly Recorder & General Advertiser 100
Big Time 50
Bill Dutton 82-84
Bill Pyers 75
Billy Barton 84
Billy Hammett 77-78
Billy Nevett 66, 123-124, 128

Billy Smallwood 124
Birmingham 22
Bishop Burton 11, 17-18, 35, 37

Bishop Burton Stakes   11
Blacklock   40
Blakesware Gold   113
Blink Bonny   11-12
Bloomsbury   36
Boleyn Castle   53
Bolivov   44
Bond Boy   49
Boroughbridge   100
Boston Spa   42
Bouchette   68
Bradford   99, 122
Bramham Moor   41, 99
Brandesburton   100
Breadalbane   12
Brecongill Stables   87-88
Brian Connorton   75, 114,
130-131

Brian Fletcher   128
Brian Henry   114, 120
Brian Rothwell   6
Bridlington   21, 42,
66, 101

Bridlington Quay Handicap
101

Brough   13, 112
Brownie Carslake   48
Bryan Smart   47, 49
Buenos Ayres   34
Bullings Hill   15
Burnby   36
Burton Agnes Stud   41-43
Burton Pidsea   32
Butterfly   35
Buxted Chickens   46
Cab on Target   138
Cambridgeshire Handicap
32

Captain Charles Frederick
Elsey   71

Captain Cobourne   106
Captain D'arcy   33
Captain James Octavious
Machell   19
Captain James Storrie   74
Captain Jennison Shafto
106

Captain S.C Henderson
77

Captain T.L Wickham-
Boynton   42
Captain Vernon   106
Carnaby   11, 44
Carnaby Stud   44
Caspar Netsher   128
Catterick   21, 36,
94, 121, 136, 142

Catwick   36
Cave Warrior   115
Celestial Cloud   47
Cesarewitch   74, 87,
113

Chapeltown Moor   104
Chaplin's Club   134
Charles Maxstead   31
Charlie Hall   88, 141
Cheb's Lad   115
Chester   32-33,
35, 68, 109, 139

Chester Cup   32, 109,
139

Chiang   146
Chris Catlin   49
Chris Thornton   46, 70
Christopher Jackson   36
Christopher Sykes   19, 39-
40

Chris Walker 4
Clare Balding 90, 113
Clifford Moor 99
Cliff Stud 46-47
Clincher 62
Clive Brittain 121
Cock of the North 109, 123
Colin Mathison 108
Colonel Lyde 70
Colonel WHH Broadley 19
Comedy King 44
Copgrove Hall Stud 46
Cottage Hospital 22
Cottingham 43, 80
County Tipperary 73
Craven Park 125
Crowther Harrison 43
Crystal Spirit 144
Dakota 46
Dale Gibson 4
Dalton Park 137
Dante 70, 75, 115, 124
David Bergin 6
David Chapman 134
David Mould 128
David O'Meara 6
Dawson Waugh 125
Deeside 48
Derby Day 48, 81
Dewhurst Stakes 40, 80, 87
Dick Curran 83
Didcot 34
Dobson Peacock 116
Dominion Royale 51
Doncaster Bloodstock Sales 53-54
Doncaster Cup 40, 44, 48, 62

Double Rose 138
Doug Smith 128
Driffield 11, 18, 32, 39, 41-42, 58-59, 79, 99, 103
Dublin Taxi 51
Duke of Clarence 102
Duke of Hamilton 20, 102
Duke of Norfolk 73, 107
Duke of Westminster 35, 40
Dutch Gold 51, 115
Earl of Derby 59
Earl of Durham 56
Easingwold 15
East Dene 108
Eastenders 132
Eboracum 98
Ebor Handicap 40, 74, 125, 139
Eclipse Stakes 40, 69, 123
Eddie Hide 128
Eddie Larkin 128
Edgar Britt 72-73, 109
Edinburgh 54, 71
Edward Petre 59, 92-93
Egton Bent 99
Elch Elder 48
Eldoret 122
Elusive Bonus 6
Emmerdale 132
Epsom 35, 37, 43, 51, 53, 59, 61, 75, 117-119, 121, 128

Eric Apter 76, 142
Escorial 144-145
Ethel Finn 117
Etton 19, 104, 126
Etton Rectory 19
Evander 17
Evichstar 74
Exeter 77
Filey 101
Finch Mason 33
Findon 19
First World War 26, 72, 93
Fitzwilliam Trust 89
Forgive 'n Forget 73
Francis Lee 49
Frank Collinson 36
Frankel 3
Frankie Dettori 53
Frank Marson 33
Fred Archer 18, 20, 94, 96, 116
Freddie Maxwell 81
Freebooter 128
Fusion 13
Game Star 123
Garrowby Stud 45
Gay Monarch 130
Geoffrey Brooke 109
Geoff Toft 69, 115, 122
George Bloss 19
George Habbershaw 86
George Reveley 137
George Robinson 44
George Smelt 15
German Governments 54
Gimcrack Stakes 128, 144

Ginger McCain 129
Gloucestershire 57
G Oates 35
Godolphin 134
Gold Aura 126
Good Hand 108
Goodwood 49, 53, 69, 79, 132
Graham Orange 4
Grand National 33-34, 48, 53, 73-74, 84, 126, 128-129
Great Rock 70
Grove Cottage Stable 83
Gunner B 67, 69-70, 122-123
Guy Reed 46, 88
Habton Grange 109, 138
Haigh Park Racecourse 105
Haisthorpe Hall 101
Halifax 45, 99, 123
Hambleton 15-16, 45, 47, 55-56, 95
Harrogate 99
Harry Carling 22
Haydock 53, 69, 89, 119
Hednesford 57, 78
Hedon 102
Helmsley 19, 47, 99
Henry Beeby 54, 143
Henry Cecil 47, 69, 123
Henry Chaplin 19

Henry Cholmondeley 43
Henry Robinson 44
Her Majesty the Queen 41, 80, 90, 140

Hermit 19-20
Heslington Boy 113
Hexham 77, 129
Hilary Jack 4, 85
Holderness 11, 41, 71, 103, 126, 137

Holderness Hunt 11, 126, 137

Hollyoaks 132
Hornsea 15
Horse and Jockey 17, 73
Horse Writers & Photographers Association 133

Howden 54
Hudson's Corner 12
Hull 2, 4-5, 22, 28, 41, 43, 47, 51, 55-56, 80, 86, 102, 125, 133-136

Hull Daily Mail 2, 4, 51, 133, 135

Hull Paragon Station 102
Hunmanby 103
Hunsley House Stud 48-49

Ian Balding 4, 113, 143

Imperieuse 11
India 109, 115
Inheritor 16
Injured Jockey's Fund 7
International Stakes 98

Jack Berry MBE 88
Jack Colling 122
Jack Jarvis 124
Jackson Group 86
James Adams 32
James "Jim" Snowden 34, 35, 101

James 'Jimmy' Thompson 64
James Melrose 98
James Voase Rank 47
Jamie Osborne 80
J Hopkinson 15
Jill Banks 4, 51-52
Jimmy Etherington 13, 50, 71

Jimmy Power 128
Jimmy the Singer 51
Job Marson 32, 61
Jodami 74
Joe Mercer 69, 111
Joe Sime 126
John Bowes 59-60
John Chapleo 4, 76
John Francome 6
John Gosden 119
John Gully 57
John Lowe 112, 138
John Mooney 4
John Orton 98
John Osborne 102
John Porter 40, 116
John Reid 53
John Scott 11, 21, 57, 59-60, 62

John Sexton 1
John Simons Harrison 43
Johnstone and Gleeson 26
John Sutcliffe 51
John Watts 43
Jonny's Joker 49
Josey Little 34

Juddmonte Stakes 3
Julio Mariner 121
Justice Keene 108
Kala Shikari 51
Karl Burke 70
Kate Walton 88
Kayudee 74
Keith Dalgleish 53
Ken Oliver 53
Kevin Keegan 49
Kevin Ryan 47, 109
Kieran Fallon 14
Kingsclere 116, 143
Kingston upon Hull 43, 47
Kiplingcotes 85, 104
Kirbymoorside 99
Lady Bayardo 22
Lady Manton 82, 131
Lady Sykes 41
La Gucaracha 46
Langton Wold 60, 105
Leconfield 7
Leeds 88-89, 99-100, 105, 135
Leicester 78, 107
Le Johnstan 51
Len Heseltine 15
Leonard Jewison 32
Lester Piggott 13-14, 46, 71, 84, 89, 115-116, 128, 145
Lewes 18
Lincoln 40, 45, 74, 125
Linda Ramsden 127
Lingfield Park 121

Little Owl 138-139
Little Weighton 48
Liverpool 17, 76, 117-118, 125
Liverpool Spring Meeting 117
Liz Hall 46
Lochnager 71
Lockington 18, 52
Londesborough Wold Farm 104
London 54, 59, 76, 81, 111, 132
Lord and Lady Halifax 45
Lord George Bentinck 45
Lord Hotham 137
Lord Irwin 30, 45
Lord John Oaksey 1, 6
Lord Manton 81, 130-131
Lucius Septimus Severus 98
Lucky Brief 75, 115
Lurine Brotherton 128
Macer Gifford 128
Major Fred Sneyd 122
Major Hudson 50
Malcolm Jefferson 119
Malcolm Tomlinson 4
Malton 4, 6-7, 11, 13, 21, 35-36, 41-42, 50, 52-53, 57-59, 61, 68, 72-74, 80, 82-83, 88-89, 105-106, 109, 114-115, 118-119, 121, 125, 128, 134, 137-138
Mark Birch 4, 139
Mark Dwyer 74

Mark Masterman Sykes   132
39

Marquis of Hastings   19-20
Marshcress   37
Marson Family   61
Mary Reveley   6, 113
Mary Rohan   4
Mathew Peacock   47, 124

Maurice Avison   6
Maurice Camacho   6, 88, 114-115

Max Gambles   112
Meaux   58
Melbourne   11, 37, 44-45

Melbourne Cup   44
Melton Vasey   136
Mennon   18
Merry Hampton   43-44
Michael Bell   127
Michael Howard   108
Mick Channon   49
Mick Easterby   50, 121, 129, 140, 143
Middleham   36-37, 65, 72, 79, 87-88, 92, 99, 110, 116, 124-125

Middle Park   40
Milk it Mick   50, 80
Miss Agnes   40
Miss Susan Michael   12
Misu Bond   50
Monsieur Bond   50
Morpeth   21
Morston   121-122

Mount Pleasant   18
Mountview Theatre School

Mr C Baxter   32
Mr Charles Buckton   50
Mr J Robinson   11
Mr Kettlewell   71
Mr R.P. Botterill   13
Mrs A.C Straker   71
Mrs Anne Henson   4
Mrs McArdy   71, 121

Musidora   72, 144-145

Musley Bank   6
My Old Dutch   51
Nancy   32-33, 35, 61

National Hunt   11, 42, 53, 74, 77, 80, 82, 93, 95, 97-98, 105-106, 119, 130, 139

Newmarket   9, 13, 20, 44, 53, 57, 65, 67, 69, 72, 74, 80, 85, 87, 94, 104, 109, 114-116, 122-123, 125, 127

Newminster   36
Nicky Connorton   115
Nidd Hall   46, 88
Nigel Tinkler   108
Night Nurse   139
Nimbus   72
Noel Cannon   48
Noel Murless   47
Norman Bertie   114
Northallerton   99
North Bar Street   10
North Grimston   21
North Yorkshire   6-7, 32, 35, 37, 50, 53, 59, 61, 88-89, 93, 137-138, 146

Norton   10, 13,
50, 59, 61, 89

Norton Grove Stud 50
Nottingham   45
Nunnington   32, 99
Oaksey House   89
Ocean Swell   124
Old Red   113
Orme   40
Ormonde   40
Ottringham   99
Ouborough Stud   47
Our Ginger   51
Outwood   107
Owthorpe   99
Paddy Broderick   139
Pan   37
Papal Bull   128
Pappa Fourway   83, 111
Parbleu   78
Park Farm, Rise   50
Park Hill Stakes   11
Pat Eddery   74, 127
Pat Rohan   68, 81,
83, 125

Pat Taylor   13, 63,
65, 85, 89, 120

Paul Blockley   80
Paul Downey   4, 68
Paul McCartney   76
Paul Midgeley   80
Paul Thorpe   4
Paymaster   103
Pearls a Singer   127
Pedalostitis   129
Penitent   13, 38,
63, 65

Percy Vasey   136
Perth   132
Peter Boddy   108

Peter Easterby   52, 109,
145

Peter Niven   138
Peter Simple   33-34
Peter Ward   51, 78,
114

Pia   121
Pickering   35, 99
Pocklington   34, 36-
37, 49, 101

Point to Point   137
Polished Steel   83
Pontefract   40, 93,
96, 145

Prince George   33
Prince Monololu   5
Queen Alexandra   117
Queen Anne   41
Quito   134
Racing Calendar   10, 93
Racing Post   135
Racing U.K   135
Radio Humberside 135
Rapid Lad   38
Raymond Simons Harrison
44

Redcar   6, 53,
86, 88, 93-94, 110, 135, 139

Reg Bond   49
Richard Eastwood   35
Richard Fahey   6, 68,
90, 119, 127, 134

Richard Hills and Hong
Richard Lingwood 50
Richard Watt   17
Richmond   35, 37,
61, 136

Right Boy 83
Rise Park 41, 99
R.M James 98
Robert B Massey 86
Robert Hill 61
Robert Morley 81
Robert Norton 10
Robert Ridsdale 57
Robert Stephenson 61
Robert Winston 53
Robin Moverley 4
Rockingham 18
Rockingham Arms 18
Roger de Stuteville 42
Ron Barnes 113
Ron Grantham 4, 28
Ron Thompson 51
Rossy Brothers 135
Royal Standard Public House 67, 69
Ruffler 41
Rum Lad 52
Rupert Watson 81, 130
Russborough 62
R.W. Armstrong 37
Sailormaite 14
Salisbury 47-48
Sally Iggulden 31
Sam Hall 70, 125
Sandiacre 84
Sandown Park 84, 131
Saucy Kit 138
Sayajirao 110
Scarborough 55, 62, 66, 106
Scotland 41, 72, 106, 113, 132
Scottish Grand National 73-74
Scottish Union 47

Sea Pigeon 109, 138-139
Settrington 53
Sewerby Cliffs 101
Shadwell 105
Sheffield 99
Shergar 46
She's Smart 52
Shirley Heights 45
Shotgun 46
Sidney Herbert 44
Sidney Renton 31, 86
Silver Stick 130
Simon Walker 126
Singapore 115
Sir Eric Ohlson 124
Sir John Renwick 74
Sir Joseph Hawley 61, 63
Sir Lycett Green 57, 77
Sir Michael Stoute 128
Sir Pertinox 39
Sir Tatton Sykes 19, 21, 39-40, 58
Skelton Moor 105
Skirlaugh 47, 50
Sledmere 19, 39-41, 58
Sledmere House 39
Smart Hostess 52-53
Smart Predator 52-53
Snowball 57
Snowy Wainwright 146
So Careful 141
Somnus 139
Soraya 63
Spigot Lodge 70, 88
Stanley Mathews 78
Stapleton Park 59
Star Cottage Stable 88
Steve Borsberry 38
Steve Cauthen 111-112

Steve Lawes 4, 68
Stewards 49, 73, 112, 134, 140-141, 146

St Giles 57
St Leger 11, 17-18, 32, 36-37, 39-40, 44, 47, 51, 54, 58-59, 61-62, 70, 72, 92, 96, 103, 110-111, 121, 139, 142

Stockton Races 16
Stokesley 99
Stuart Webster 14
Sunacelli 75
Superior Class 68
Sydney 109
Tadcaster 99
Talbot Hotel 106
Teddington 61, 63
Teleprompter 43
The Aire & Calder Navigation Company 105
The Belvoir 82
The Cure 40
The Duke of Montrose 19
The House that Jack Built 89

Thirsk 63, 68, 95-96, 130, 138

Thomas Field 37
Thoroughbred Stud 43
Tibthorpe 58
Tiddlewinks 46
Tiger Inn 10
Tim Molony 82, 128-129

Tipperary Tim 84
Tip the Wink 64
Tollerton 99
Tom Cunningham 33-34

Tom Lister 33
Tommy Dent 78
Tommy Ellerington 101
Tommy Tittlemouse 18
Tommy Walsh 115
Tommy Weldon 37
Tom Oliver 34
Tom Stebbing Green 55
Tony Ives 146
Tranby Croft 102
Treasure Hunter 113
Triple Crown 40, 45, 59, 117

Tunstall 99
Unknown Quantity 72
Vintage Premium 119
Vivacious Boy 134
Vulcan 101
Wally Swinburn 112
Warpath 46
Warrington 116, 118
Waterloo 43, 90, 121

Watt Memorial Plate 17-18

Watton 32
Wawne Church 58
West Australian 45, 59
Weymouth 39
Whitewall Stables 59
Whitsbury Stud 48
William 'Bill' Scott 57
William Derby 98
William Edward Elsey 71
William Goater 19
William Hill 49, 121
William Thornton 56
William Thorpe 47
Willie Stephenson 53
Winston Churchill 124
Withernsea 107

Wokingham Stakes 51
Woodhouse Moor 105
World War Two 65
Wright Stakes 61
Wyndham 16
Ya Malak 118
Yapham Mill Stud 49-50
York 3, 5, 15,
23, 34, 39, 45-46, 53, 57, 63,
66, 69-70, 74-77, 81, 84, 87,
90-91, 94, 97-98, 100, 108,
114-115, 118-119, 122, 128,
130, 144-145

Yorkshire Oaks 99
Yorkshire Post 135
Zetland 61, 62,
87